"With candid points, clear illustrations, insightful commentary, and helpful discussion questions, this book is a powerful resource for congregations who desire new life."
—Tom Berlin, Lead Pastor, Floris United Methodist Church, Herndon, VA

"In today's ministry context, people must be unleashed for service. Yet, sometimes outdated church systems and 'we've never done it that way' attitudes stifle bold and innovative ministry. In *Just Say Yes!* Bishop Schnase insightfully helps leaders break out of old thinking to help set people free for fruitful ministry. Every ministry leader would do well to read, absorb, and apply his or her practical insight."
—Charles Stone, Lead Pastor, West Park Church, London, Ontario, Canada; author of *Brain-Savvy Leaders* from Abingdon Press

"*Just Say Yes!* gave me practical tools and encouragement to be a leader who says *Yes* and empowers others to do the same."
—Jacob Armstrong, Lead Pastor, Providence United Methodist Church, Mt. Juliet, TN; author, *The New Adapters* from Abingdon Press

"Bishop Schnase's life, ministry, and mission are rooted in empowering and unleashing pastors, churches, and their leaders so that they grow together to accomplish abundantly far more than anything they could ask or imagine. Schnase's vision for the church in *Just Say Yes!* is compelling and necessary for pastors and laity who are looking to be bold and take risks as they continue in the work of building up communities of faith for the sake of transforming the world. This book is a great read!"
—Scott Chrostek, Pastor, The United Methodist Church of the Resurrection Downtown Campus, Kansas City, MO

JUST say YES!

JUST say YES!

Other Books by Robert Schnase

Seven Levers: Missional Strategies for Conferences
The Fruitful Living Series
Remember the Future: Praying for the Church and Change
Practicing Extravagant Generosity: Daily Readings on the Grace of Giving
Forty Days of Fruitful Living: Practicing a Life of Grace
Five Practices of Fruitful Living
The Balancing Act: A Daily Rediscovery of Grace
Cultivating Fruitfulness: Five Weeks of Prayer and Practice for Congregations
Five Practices of Fruitful Congregations
Ambition in Ministry: Our Spiritual Struggle with Success, Achievement,
and Competition
Testing and Reclaiming Your Call to Ministry

Abingdon Press is honored to publish these and other Robert Schnase books. Visit your favorite bookseller or Cokesbury.com to place an order.

Robert Schnase

Author of *Five Practices of Fruitful Congregations*

JUST
say

YES!

UNLEASHING PEOPLE
FOR MINISTRY

Abingdon Press™

Nashville

JUST SAY YES!
UNLEASHING PEOPLE FOR MINISTRY

Copyright © 2015 by Robert Schnase

All rights reserved.

This book is printed on acid-free paper.

Library of Congress Cataloging-in-Publication Data

Just say yes! : unleashing people for ministry / Robert Schnase.—First [edition].
   pages cm
Includes bibliographical references.
ISBN 978-1-4267-7613-7 (binding: pbk.)   1. Church renewal.   2. Change—Religious aspects—Christianity.   I. Title.
   BV600.3.S3535 2015
   253—dc23

                                                              2015000816

Scripture quotations unless noted otherwise are from the Common English Bible. Copyright © 2011 by the Common English Bible. All rights reserved. Used by permission. www.CommonEnglishBible.com.

Scripture quotations from THE MESSAGE. Copyright © by Eugene H. Peterson 1993, 1994, 1995, 1996, 2000, 2001, 2002. Used by permission of NavPress Publishing Group.

15 16 17 18 19 20 21 22 23 24—10 9 8 7 6 5 4 3 2 1

MANUFACTURED IN THE UNITED STATES OF AMERICA

Introduction

Warning! This is a dangerous book. Used properly, ideas contained in this book can lead to an explosion of ministry! Proceed with care.

Just Say Yes! Unleashing People for Ministry is written for people whose passion has been simmering for years, who yearn to be told *Yes!* It's for those whose energy and ideas have been tamped down by systems and attitudes that restrain ministry, and who have felt frustrated by attempts to start new programs, reach new people, or experiment with alternative worship services, only to be told *No*. This book sets disciples free, giving them the permission to be bold and fruitful in their following of Christ. *Just Say Yes!* helps us give one another greater courage for the purposes of Christ. *Just Say Yes!* helps churches get unstuck.

The church says *No* in a thousand ways to new ideas, ministry initiatives, and creative people. Pastors say *No* to the ideas of laity, and lay persons say *No* to the initiatives of pastors. Committees say *No* to staff, and staff say *No* to volunteers. Long-established members say *No* to new people, and traditional worshippers say *No* to contemporary worshippers. Existing classes, mission teams, and music ministries greet new initiatives with suspicion and resistance.

When *No* pervades a congregation, people find a hundred reasons why a new idea won't work, and so the congregation accepts the default of doing things the way they've always done them before. Mission initiatives, service projects, justice ministries, alternative worship expressions, children's programs, and bold inspirations to start new classes, small groups, or second sites—all fall victim to *No*. People who sense a calling to serve feel restrained and shut out rather than encouraged and supported. *No* stifles ministry, kills innovation, and deadens enthusiasm.

Most churches struggle with antiquated systems that are no longer conducive to our mission, which have the effect of saying *No*. New ideas face systemic resistance because of the labyrinth of committees, steps, and policies that become impossible to navigate and which cause excruciating frustration and delay. Systems that merely irritate long-standing leaders create insurmountable obstacles to younger generations who have little tolerance for our bewildering approach toward ministry. An unrelenting culture of *No* is a contradiction to our sacrament of baptism, stifling hope, new birth, and a sense of God's promise for the future.

Successful congregations are willing to take action that declining churches are unwilling to do. Growing churches say *Yes* to ministries that declining churches say *No* to. Missional churches shift a *No* culture to a culture that helps people cultivate their calling and creativity.

People need to be unleashed for ministry—encouraged and emboldened, equipped and sent out. Unleashed means to set free, to unbind from restraint, to set loose. Churches that unleash people for ministry rethink their operations, focus on the way God calls everyone to ministry, and reduce the resistance that holds people back from taking initiative. They create a culture of *Yes*, of cultivating God's call to diverse expressions of ministry. They expect people to have good ideas for ministry, and they realize that new ideas can come from anywhere or anyone. They eliminate unnecessary obstacles. They unfetter laity and staff from those systems that restrain them from using their creativity and gifts. They practice the ministry of encouragement.

Unleashed also means "to set forcefully in motion," such as when a medical discovery unleashes a host of new cures or a technical breakthrough unleashes a rush of new innovations. When we set people free to do the work of God, the spirit of Christ propels us into places and into ministries we could never have imagined.

How do we set people free for ministry? How do we help people fulfill their callings to teach, lead, and serve? How do we develop a permission-giving church? That's what this book is about.

Just Say Yes! Unleashing People for Ministry helps pastors and congregational leaders examine the systems, attitudes, and dynamics that restrain, control, and diminish ministry. This book provides suggestions for how to become a permission-giving congregation and describes the changes in values, attitudes, and behaviors that lead a congregation out of stagnation and toward an outward-focused, missional culture that's willing to try new expressions of ministry in order to fulfill the mission of Christ.

Just Say Yes! is written to offer hope and inspiration for congregations that want to become more fruitful, adept at initiating ministry, and open to innovation for the purposes of Christ.

Use the ideas and examples as a catalyst for conversations among staff, with lay leadership, for planning retreats, and with councils and teams that oversee ministry. The book provides a resource for pastors to reflect upon their congregational systems and their own leadership styles, and to discuss them with other pastors. The book gives leaders of lay training events a way to rethink where ideas for ministry come from and how they are received, supported, and evaluated.

Like *Five Practices of Fruitful Congregations, Just Say Yes!* is written in an accessible, practical style for use with a wide audience, including adult Sunday school classes, small group studies, planning task forces, and those who lead volunteer teams, mission projects, youth work, and outreach ministries.

I do not write this as an expert or consultant. You won't find formulas to follow, models to replicate, or how-to's to check off. I draw attention to things that we ordinarily don't notice in the systems we use and the attitudes we harbor. In my own following of Christ, I desire to become more intentionally an encourager of ministry rather than a person who unknowingly contributes to systems that restrain or discourage initiative for Christ. I hope this book causes churches to remove as many constraints, distractions, and obstacles to ministry as possible so that people can thrive in serving Christ. I pray that congregations can loosen up, come alive to the mission of Christ with greater boldness, and discover the delight that comes when we use our gifts for God's purposes.

I hope reading this book changes your church, and changes something in you, so that you feel greater freedom to offer yourself wholeheartedly to Christ and to encourage others to do so as well.

Chapter One

You Can't Do It
That Way

People Who Say *No*

The ministry at Pastor Janelle's church was thriving. She had arrived three years earlier to serve a congregation that struggled with finances, an aging membership, unaddressed facility repairs, and years of slow decline. Her passion, energy, focus, hard work, and gifted preaching had helped stimulate a resurgence of ministry. Families were joining the church, and an array of successful small group ministries, Bible studies, and mission initiatives reached more and more people. People were growing in discipleship and service with a contagious excitement about serving Christ and the world around them. Trust in Janelle's leadership was high, finances were positive, and continued growth seemed inevitable.

So it came as a surprise to Janelle when her suggestion to start a new worship service with a different music style was greeted with such immediate objection. Her conversations with younger members convinced her that the church could extend its ministry and reach more people by offering an alternative worship service in addition to the traditional one. She studied how other congregations launched services, and prayed and planned before presenting the idea. People with the musical gifts to lead such a service already participated in the church and were prepared to offer their leadership. Everything seemed right, and the time seemed ripe.

Nearly everyone she presented her idea to said *No*.

The regular attendees complained that the new service would take people from the old service. Two services would divide the congregation and create the feel of two different churches.

The greeters and ushers said *No*, expressing concern about the extra volunteer time required to cover another service. The hospitality team said *No* because they would need to recruit more people to serve at the welcome table.

1

The part-time music director said *No* because nobody had asked her opinion earlier, and the music at the new service wasn't her style. She also objected because the new service might take singers from her choir.

The worship committee worried about how two services with different liturgical and music styles would affect the way the congregation offered their Christmas Eve service.

The secretary resisted because she'd have to create two different bulletins and keep track of two sets of registration pads. She also felt hurt that the pastor had not consulted her before sharing the ideas with others. The nursery coordinator was upset because she'd need to schedule additional volunteers.

The trustees signaled *No* because of the necessity of moving sound equipment in and out of the worship space each week. The finance committee resisted because of the additional staffing costs for the nursery and musicians.

Sunday school teachers were upset thinking the new service might interrupt attendance patterns, causing some families to take their children out of class. Even the good-hearted volunteers who count the offering complained about needing to be present for an additional service.

The wide-spread resistance caught Janelle off guard. All the literature on growing churches and her own research, prayer, and intuition told her that a well-led additional worship service would help the church grow, and yet everyone seemed resistant or downright opposed to the idea. Leaders agreed with the priority of reaching more people, and loved their pastor, but virtually everyone found a reason why the new service was not a good idea.

New ministry ideas elicit more *No* reactions than *Yes* responses regardless of how good the idea is, how missional the focus, how promising the prospects of success, or who initially presents the idea.

Can we start a Bible study for young adults?
Can we offer a divorce recovery group?
Can we form a team of volunteers to take a weekly shift at the
    homeless shelter?
Can the youth hold a fund-raiser?
Can our church adopt a refugee family?
Can Alcoholics Anonymous meet here?
Can middle-school children serve as ushers and greeters?
Can we put coloring books in the foyer for children during
    worship?

Can we form a praise band?

Can we train an emergency response team to help following natural disasters?

Most of what lay people hear in the church to questions like these is *No, No, No*. Many pastors and staff members hear the same from their members, just as Janelle did. In fact, people expect the church to say *No*.

Where do the *No*'s come from? Everywhere. A thousand reasons are expressed why any new idea is rejected. In some churches, people are so polite that no one actually explicitly says *No*, but the hesitancies, questions, and second-guessing foster an unmistakable restraint that slows forward motion. As one volunteer trying to get a ministry launched said, "I feel like I'm walking through knee-deep molasses with leaden shoes!"

The Ways People Say *No*

The following list is an attempt to express the ways people say *No* to other people. Every one of these has happened in churches, and some of these behaviors and attitudes I've discovered in myself. Here are some of the ways people say *No*:

You're Not the Pastor. Many ministry ideas are rejected by the pastor because of the belief that only clergy can lead a particular form of ministry or have the discernment to determine what ministries the church should offer. The pastor has to be the one to teach the Bible study, to lead a prayer service, to visit the hospital, or to call on prospective members. Only the pastor can lead membership classes or teach confirmation. The senior pastor insists on being the only person on staff who can conduct weddings and funerals. These beliefs, held by many lay members as well, limit the growth of the church and the exercise of ministry. Ordained or licensed pastors, and the seminary education that prepares them, are important for leading the church, but they are not essential to the practice of ministry. If we limit new ministries only to those that the clergy initiate, plan, and lead, we restrict the capacities of the church to a fraction of what otherwise could be accomplished for the purposes of Christ. Far more ministries can be done, and should be done, by called, trained, and passionate laity than are usually permitted or encouraged.

A subtle clergy-centered attitude provides unseen downward pressures on creativity. Many highly gifted laypersons begin to work in response to a genuine calling, only to discover that instead of receiving the blessing of their pastor, they experience resistance or control. Pastors deaden the impulse of their most creative people by needing to be at the center of everything.

I Don't Need That, So Why Should We Do It? A few people desire to launch a ministry, and they bring their idea to the church council. Most on the council have no interest in the new worship service or the Bible study because their spiritual needs are being met. If the proposal is put to a vote, the council may say *No* simply because the majority of people present have no need for such a ministry.

Only Five People Signed Up. Leaders say *No* because they oppose initiating a ministry that doesn't involve a sufficiently large number of people.

But how many people does it take to have a meaningful Bible study that can help people grow in grace and in love for God? Fifty? Fifteen? If only two people meet for lunch each week, read together a chapter of scripture, discuss it, and pray for one another, they will be strengthened.

The same is true for most ministry ideas. Some ministries start small and stay small, but meet real needs. Others start small and slowly grow to include more people. Some come and go quickly, but nevertheless serve a purpose in the lives of those who participate. Only twelve people originally signed up to follow Jesus as disciples, and one of those backed out at the last minute!

They're Not Our Members Anyway. Many congregations believe that the ministries of the church are for us, for our friends, and for our children and grandchildren. Why do we offer Vacation Bible School? So that *our* children can learn the faith. Ideas to reach children or families who have no church connection are rejected. Basketball leagues are prevented from using the facility, soccer teams are prohibited from using the property, and scout troops are kept out of the building because they aren't our children. Playgrounds have signs and fences and locks that keep neighborhood kids away.

Very few assumptions are more crippling to the mission of the church.

That's Our Room. People say *No* because the space that would best host the proposed ministry is already used by another group for another purpose at another time! "They can't put children in there on Wednesday nights because that's the Wesley Bible Study's room on Sunday morning!" Contentiousness over rooms, meeting times, and setting up and taking down tables limits more ministry than we realize.

That Will Never Work Here (and I'll See That It Doesn't!). Sometimes the council approves a new ministry over the objection or without consultation with the staff or volunteers who play critical roles in daily operations. A positive vote by the council, however, does not mean that everyone will suddenly become eager to help, and a musician who doesn't want to sing at the new service can send a thousand signals of his or her discontent, creating discomfort or awkwardness for everyone.

A secretary who doesn't like being bothered by all the inquiries about a ministry that she doesn't support becomes an obstacle by her unwillingness to give helpful answers for those wanting to participate.

Passive aggressive behavior, a negative attitude, snide remarks, or the simple unwillingness to follow through can cast a shadow on the entire ministry. Snarky remarks by a staff member can poison the experience of volunteers. When people resent the inconvenience a ministry is causing them, they may hope that the initiative fails. They may act as silent saboteurs, and will stand ready to say "I told you so" when the program does not succeed.

They Can Just Join Us. Suppose young adults want to form their own Bible study or start an alternative worship service, or that newcomers want to adopt a mission project. A common response from existing Bible study leaders, attendees of the current service, or team members of the on-going mission projects is to say, "Why can't they join us?"

Church growth experts agree that new people join new groups more easily than existing groups. Pressuring people to come to existing ministries rather than starting their own disguises an underlying sentiment that says, "You can belong here as long as you do things the way we do them, and like things the way we like them."

Analysis Paralysis. People say *No* by demanding answers to questions that no one can know how to answer before a project is approved and first steps are taken. Leaders kill an idea by a paralyzing demand for data, for information and outcomes and consequences and contingencies that cannot be known beforehand. Leaders may work on the false assumption that more information will assure certainty of outcomes, and so they focus excessively on a demand for more research, measurement, study, analysis, and data. How would this work? What if you don't get enough money? What if too few people sign up? What if too many attend? What if it rains? What if, what if what if…?

When we require answers to every possible contingency before we proceed, we never move forward. Ultimately, data is not as persuasive as narrative, experience, anecdote, and story. The essence of faith is captured in the words that describe Abraham's obedience to God's call, "He went out without knowing where he was going" (Heb 11:8).

You're Too Young, Too New, or Too Different. Some churches have an unwritten rule that someone must belong to the church for several years before their ideas and opinions are taken seriously. They have to earn their right to lead positive change. And yet, often newcomers offer the freshest and most accurate perspective on the practices of a congregation. They have not yet grown accustomed and acculturated to the old ways, and they can better see the contradictions and inconsistencies of current practices. Good ideas come from everywhere and everyone—young and old, newcomers and old-timers, the experienced and the novice.

You're Doing It All Wrong. Sometimes the way people say *No* has little to do with votes on committees or decisions by leaders. You can sense disapproval, suspicion, and negativity in their demeanor before they ever say a word.

Some faces carry a countenance of *No*, and other faces say *Yes*. Some looks say, "We're glad you're here!" and others say, "What do you think you're doing here?" Some say, "Let me help you with that," and others say, "Don't you know anything about how things work here?"

Disparaging remarks, harsh corrections, disapproving glances, the shaking of the head and the crossing of the arms—these scream *No* louder than anything else the church may say or do. These actions tear down rather than build up; they provide demolition rather than edification.

A young woman became involved with a church and began to offer her time to help in small ways. For her, these were big steps, uncertain and tentative. She signed up to provide refreshments for a Wednesday evening children's ministry, and this took her into the church kitchen for the first time. She searched through drawers and cabinets looking for what she needed, and eventually found plastic plates and glasses and began to set things up. No sooner had she completed preparations than a longstanding member of the kitchen team arrived and scolded her for doing everything wrong, saying she had no business in the kitchen without an experienced member of the kitchen team. She gathered up the plates and glasses, put them away, and told the newcomer that she wished the church had locks on these cabinets to keep people out. She then stepped into a closet near the kitchen and pointed out the proper utensils and plates for the children. She walked away shaking her head.

The newcomer had to fight back tears as she continued to lay out the refreshments. She felt embarrassed and humiliated. She never volunteered again, and drifted away from the church. Demolition. She was told *No* in the loudest and clearest way.

This is a true story. So is the experience of the mom who visited worship for the first time with her infant daughter. When the baby squealed, the woman behind her learned forward and whispered, "Sometimes the sermons have that same effect on me!" She slipped forward into the seat beside the visitor and offered to help by walking the baby in the foyer. After the service, she introduced the young mother to the nursery director and showed her the rocking chairs at the back of the sanctuary for parents with babies. Encouragement. Edification. *Yes*, incarnated.

A similar dynamic emerges when someone musters enough courage to suggest a new ministry idea. A sense of calling begins with vulnerability, self-consciousness, and uncertainty. New ideas are like the flickering flame of a candle, capable of being extinguished with the slightest breath. A countenance of *No* can end initiative before it has a chance.

You Didn't Ask Me First. Ideas are disregarded because the pastor or a particular lay leader or a church staff member was not involved in the original conversations. Senior pastors quash the work of staff members because they weren't consulted, or lay leaders refuse to support a project because they weren't asked to serve on the planning team.

Imagine having such a robust ministry that not even the pastor knows everything that's going on! In contrast, I've known pastors and laypersons who felt genuinely hurt if they didn't know every detail of every activity. We can do better.

Don't Rock the Boat. People say *No* because they are afraid that someone will not approve or will disagree or otherwise feel offended by the launch of the new ministry. Someone might complain because of the costs, the people invited to lead it, the visibility of the project, the effect on other ministries, or the jealousy that other leaders may experience. Or they fear that the new initiative will fail, and therefore people will blame the leaders who approved it.

Things Won't Be the Same. The old-timers are right in saying that the new worship service would bring change. If it succeeds, more people will become active in following Christ, people who have fundamentally different tastes in music, worship, attitudes toward service, and ideas about God. Part of the challenge is to convince existing members that reaching new people to connect them with Christ is so essential that it's worth the pain of losing some of the atmosphere and culture of the existing church.

New people bring a new day. New ministries change the church. And part of the work of leadership is constantly reminding people that change is good, and that no church will thrive unless it's willing to adapt itself to the mission field.

Why do people resist change and reject new ideas even when they know that the old habits, attitudes, and systems are holding them back from doing greater good? Ronald Heifetz says that people do not fear change; they fear loss.[1] People fear the grief that comes with losing what has been familiar, reliable, and known; habits, values, and attitudes—even those that have been barriers to progress and unhelpful for the mission—are part of one's identity, and changing them challenges how we define ourselves.

Abandoning long-held patterns feels like we are being disloyal to those who created and taught the older, familiar ways. People cling to ideas as a way of holding on to the persons who taught them the ideas. Change means leaving behind the familiar, and possibly experiencing uncertainty and incompetence with the new. No wonder people resist change!

Faulty Assumptions

Assumptions are notions or beliefs that a group accepts as true, even though they may remain unstated. Organizations operate with many unknown assumptions and follow them to make decisions about what to do. Many reasons why people say *No* derive from faulty assumptions.

This Is Our Church
The first faulty assumption is that this is our church.

To whom does the church really belong? Does the church belong to the pastor? No, even though the pastor plays a pivotal role in leading and strengthening the church.

Does the church belong to the trustees? To the church council? To the members who contributed money to build the facility? All of these make significant contributions to the operation, definition, and mission of the church.

However, at a fundamental level, the church belongs to Jesus Christ, and to Jesus Christ alone. The church is the body of Christ. The church derives its purpose from Christ, conducts its ministry in the spirit of Christ, and exists to further the revelation of God in Jesus Christ. The church connects people to Christ and represents Christ in the world. As such, the church seeks to emulate Jesus, teach the truth that Jesus teaches, serve the people Jesus serves, and love the way Jesus loves. The pastor, staff, and lay leadership serve to remind that the church belongs to Christ. They lead people in the mission of Christ. The church has no mission and purpose apart from Christ.

When we act as if the church belongs to us—the pastor, the staff, the leaders, the members—then the criteria for why we say *Yes* or *No* becomes what *we* prefer, what *we* want, what *we* seek. We insist on voting on everything that happens, and we believe that we must know everything that goes on. The more people who accept this assumption, the more convoluted the permission-withholding processes grow. We become the center rather than

Christ. We align the ministries with our preferences rather than discerning what aligns with Christ's work. We become protective, defensive, controlling, and territorial. We say *No*.

Ideas Come from the Center

A second faulty assumption is that ideas come from the center.

Picture the church as a set of concentric circles, with a small circle in the middle, surrounded by a larger circle, and then a larger circle, and so on. The small inner circle represents the insiders, including the pastor, staff, and a few laity who know nearly everything that happens. The next larger circle includes the elected chairpersons, the leaders of teams, and teachers of classes. The next circle includes those who participate in small groups and serve on teams and volunteer on committees. The next larger circle includes those who regularly attend worship. Another larger circle includes those who feel like they belong to the church even though they attend sporadically. Each larger circle includes all the people in the inner circles. At the outer edge of the largest circle, a margin delineates those who belong to the church from those who have no relationship with the church. We hope the margin is permeable so that new people can enter the community of faith easily, and we can reach out across it daily.

It's at that margin that the church fulfills its mission. It's at that margin that people who belong to the church engage other people with the evangelistic mission of the church, inviting them to explore the spiritual life. And it's at the margin that we offer our ministries of mercy, mission, service, and justice to relieve suffering, seek peace, and reconcile people. The mission of the church is not fulfilled at the center in council meetings, planning retreats, and finance committees, as important as those are. At best, these meetings prepare us for the mission.

The role of leadership in the church is to direct the attention of the church toward that margin and therefore toward the mission. If this is the case, where do the freshest and most relevant ideas come from for leading the church?

Many of the best ideas come from people at the margins rather than from leaders or the pastor. Rather than a good idea occurring in a meeting, and then leaders building congregational support from the center toward the edges, the most creative churches have managed to establish systems that provide a conduit from the edges to the center. Instead of the church council adopting a program and then convincing volunteers to implement it, a ministry begins with the sense of calling and enthusiasm among people at the margins, builds momentum, and then becomes recognized and adopted by the council.

A person discovers an unmet need, feels called to help, enlists others, and sets to work. Eventually what began as a personal calling becomes a larger ministry and is adopted as a program of the church.

The assumption that ideas must begin at the center and be controlled from the center fosters a tendency to say *No* to new ideas that come from anywhere else.

It's All about Us

A third, more subtle assumption is that it's all about us.

It's been said that when people hear a new idea, ninety-nine percent of the people, ninety-nine percent of the time, think, "What's in it for me?" It's not that those who say *No* lack commitment to Christ. Most people simply approach an idea by filtering it through the perspective of their own experience: "How does this affect me? Will I benefit from it?" And most importantly, "What will I have to do? What will it cost me?"

This natural and understandable response limits mission, stifles creativity, and squelches the genuine call of God.

Saying that the majority of people begin with "What's in it for me?" probably overstates the point, but I find the words personally convicting. When I'm asked whether I think we should go forward with an idea, if I don't monitor myself to focus on the larger mission, my default response reflects my personal preference and my perception of the impact that the decision will have on me.

But it's not about me. It's not about the pastor. It's not about the preferences of the committee. It's not about the trustees, or the building, or the members who built and lead the church. It's about Christ, and Christ alone.

The focus should be "How does this help the mission of Christ grow and multiply? Does this help us reach new or different people with the good news of Jesus Christ?"

Most of the reasons people said *No* to the plan Janelle presented had to do with the effect that launching a new service had on them. Becoming an outward-focused church shifts the energy toward the mission and away from personal preference. "What is God calling us to do?" is a fundamentally different question from, "What do I want to do?"

The combined effect of these many ways we say *No* is that we fail to initiate new ministries, shut down the inspirations and callings of our laity and clergy, and simply repeat ministries that we're already familiar with. We do things just like we've always done them.

Churches take the path of least resistance. They default to the status quo. We avoid change and revert to familiar ways of doing things. Nothing grows. Nothing adapts or evolves or improves. It is always easier to avoid starting a second worship service and to continue on as before. It's easier not to start an additional Sunday school class and not to launch an after-school tutoring program.

When we follow the path of least resistance, the church grows smaller and older with each succeeding generation, less relevant to the needs of people in the world and less engaged with the community.

We must change the default from *No*. When we say *No* more than we say *Yes*, the ministry of Christ suffers.

When lay and clergy leadership learn to believe that *Yes* is a possibility, it changes everything. They make things possible instead of assuming things can never work. They focus on the mission of Christ and the way God calls all people to ministry.

Why Is This Important?

Successful churches and effective pastors are willing to do things that declining churches and unsuccessful pastors are unwilling to do. It's that simple.

Growing churches say *Yes* to ministries that declining churches say *No* to. They have figured out how to foster creativity, nurture the call of God among their people, value innovation, and take initiative. They have learned to adapt and learn and respond and grow. They have become unstuck.

William Bridges has written extensively on change and transitions in organizations. In any significant transition, the very thing that has brought the organization to its current point is what needs to be let go of the most.[2] To move forward requires letting go of many of the practices, programs, and attitudes that met our needs, formed our identity, and that helped us reach our current point. In a strange contradiction, it's our progress with current ministries that helps us realize we have to change even more.

Leading change is difficult for leaders and requires extraordinary courage and faith. Bridges describes the profound challenges that leaders face. Those who are most at home with the way things are—those people who have been fed by the current ministries, who helped create them, and have valued and appreciated them—will be those who experience the greatest loss.

Organizations take the path of least resistance when faced with a choice. The church needs leaders able to say that Christ is calling us to take the more difficult path. Jesus is calling us to do the harder work that reaches people and changes the world rather than just those things we prefer for ourselves. Jesus calls us, not to do whatever is easiest, but to do what moves us out of our comfort zone to fulfill God's purposes.

Churches must overcome their natural tendency to take the path of least resistance. It takes courage and intentionality to shift from a culture of *No* to the culture of *Yes*.

The Long History of Telling People **No**

No is not a new word in the vocabulary of the people of God. Some of the most amazing moments in the history of our faith occurred when people called by God overcame the objections of other religious leaders, friends, and relatives.

Moses first had to overcome the voices inside himself that said *No* to God. He had several good excuses to offer God as to why he was not the person to free the Hebrew people. "No one will listen to me....I'm powerless....No one will believe me....No one will pay attention....I don't speak well" (Exod 3, paraphrase). When he led the people out of slavery, they began to question him immediately. "Why did you bring us out of Egypt to kill us?" (Exod 17:3).

Sarah and Abraham were convinced by the people around them and the voices within them who said *No* to the possibility of future generations. Jonah said *No, No, No* to the idea of reaching the people of Nineveh.

Jesus was surrounded by people who told him *No*. The scribes and Pharisees repeatedly grumbled about Jesus spending time with the tax collectors and sinners. The Sadducees said *No* to his healing people on the Sabbath. Any time he touched lepers, spent time with foreign women, told stories of Samaritans in a positive light, or interceded on behalf of the woman accused of adultery, he confronted *No* from religious leaders, followers, and kinfolk. His closest companions tried to dissuade him from going forward to Jerusalem, causing Jesus to say, "Get behind me, Satan. You are a stone that could make me stumble" (Matt 16:23).

Peter wrestled with the *No*'s that prohibited Gentiles from belonging to the followers of Christ. Paul challenged leaders who said *No* to the new Christians who approached the faith without a Jewish heritage.

John Wesley, the founder of Methodism, confronted a cacophony of *No*'s from Anglican priests, bishops, laypersons, and even his own brother as he supported field preaching, the establishment of preaching houses, the use of laypersons in ministry, the launching of Sunday schools, and the ordaining of pastors for America.

Every sanctuary you've worshipped in, every youth ministry that shaped your life, every church van you've ridden in, every music team that has caused your soul to soar, every mission project that you've volunteered for, every outreach your church has offered that has changed someone's life—all of these were begun, built, supported, and offered over the objections of people who said *No*. They came to fruition because enough leaders dared to say *Yes*.

What Legacy Will We Leave?

A member of a congregation was known for his opposition to everything. Whatever the idea, he voted *No* and worked diligently to recruit others to say *No*. He opposed every idea the pastor brought up and every change proposed by fellow members. He asked a thousand questions, lifted a hundred objections, thwarted dozens of initiatives. He would say *No* for any reason, or for no reason at all. For the congregation to move forward, they required overcoming his objections, outvoting him, or working around him. He did this for years before I knew him, and continued for years after I last spoke with him.

What a legacy! He killed ideas, closed down initiatives, curtailed the ministries of energetic and passionate people. It's sad to imagine what good might have been accomplished. He stood in the way of countless children who could have been nurtured in the faith, families that could have been reached, and elderly who could have experienced the grace of God.

Don't be that person. Don't operate with *No* as your default response to all things new. Give the Spirit room to move. Be the person God works through rather than the person God has to work around. Leave a legacy of encouragement, of support, of prayerful discernment. Unleash people for ministry.

Questions for Reflection and Discussion

1. Review the subsection entitled, "The Ways People Say *No*." Can you think of a time when you inadvertently used one of these behaviors or attitudes to express your resistance to a ministry idea?

2. Think of two or three successful ministries that have begun in your congregation in recent years. Where did the ideas come from? How were the ideas initially received? What form of resistance did the ideas face at first, and how did the ministries come to fruition anyway?

3. Where do you see *"what's in it for me?"* thinking at work in your church or community?

4. "Successful churches and effective pastors are willing to do things that declining churches and unsuccessful pastors are unwilling to do. Growing churches say *Yes* to ministries that declining churches say *No* to." Do you agree? What do you see as some of the implications of this for your congregation?

To Delve Deeper

Read Luke 6:1-11 and Matthew 9:9-13. Jesus was surrounded by people seeking to restrain him, catch him in any infraction, and otherwise say *No* to his ministry. How did Jesus respond to his critics? How did he reframe encounters in order to direct people toward the mission God sent him to fulfill? How did he empower his disciples to take bold action for God's love?

Prayer

Rescue us, Lord, from thinking first and foremost about ourselves and our preferences. Help us so live as a congregation so that your Spirit works through us to accomplish your purposes rather than working around us as obstacles to your grace. Open us to your will, and to the people and ideas that refresh the ministry of Christ among us.

Chapter Two

Committees, Rules, and Policies

Systems That Say *No*

Dana watches on television the devastation wrought by a tornado in a neighboring state. As she sees people weeping over their lost homes and their broken community, she feels called by God to do something and imagines leading a team to help people replace their homes and rebuild their lives. Dana possesses the talents to organize and lead people. She talks to friends, and several of them want to help. She tells her pastor about her belief that the church could do something that would make a difference. The project sounds like work for the mission committee, and the pastor tells Dana to take her idea to them. Unfortunately, the committee only meets four times a year and it just met last night!

So Dana meets with the mission committee a few months later and enthusiastically describes how volunteers could sleep on church floors at night and work on rooftops during the day. They could use chain saws to clear fallen trees or operate backhoes to remove debris. They might offer a Vacation Bible School for the children of families who were affected by the disaster.

The mission committee is composed of people who agreed to serve with the promise that they would only need to attend four meetings per year. They can't imagine climbing on rooftops or sleeping on floors. Their eyes grow large as Dana describes her vision. They admire Dana's passion, but they can't see themselves participating in such a robust project. They tell her that the project requires further approval from the church council. Unfortunately, the council also meets once each quarter, and they just met last week!

Dana continues to feel called to help tornado victims, and she remains persistent. Six months after the storm, she meets with the church council and they listen to her plan. They are also overwhelmed by the boldness of the proposal. One member points out that her plan requires funding for travel and supplies. The council directs Dana to meet with the finance committee the following month.

Dana patiently presents her plan to the finance committee. They determine that the project requires a change in the budget and inform Dana that such an adjustment can only be done in October when the budget is prepared for the coming year.

Eighteen months following the tornado—after the pastor, the mission committee, the church council, the finance committee, the church council again, the annual church-wide conference, the finance committee again, and the mission committee again have all heard her plans—Dana is given the go-ahead to lead a team. By then the disaster has passed and the opportunity to make a difference is lost.

Have you ever belonged to an organization that is paralyzed by its own confusing and convoluted decision-making processes?

Many congregations require five to seven layers of organizational approval, involving committees, the pastor, the church staff, the finance committee, the church council, and perhaps the vote of the entire congregation. Each person or committee has the ability to say *No*, but nobody has the authority to say *Yes*. Many of our congregational systems are not conducive to our mission. They restrain ministry rather than foster creativity.

Death by Complexity

Not only do *people* say *No* to new ideas, but *systems* say *No* when they operate in a manner that restrains, limits, and frustrates. Few ideas, if any, survive. An initiative that no one opposes and everyone supports can die because the systems are so complex, convoluted, or confusing. People never receive permission to act because our systems themselves say *No*.

Systems are the way things get done within a church. The word *system* does not imply that every step has been carefully mapped out on an organizational chart or formally agreed-upon. To the contrary, most systems have not been systematically planned.

Systems include a mix of formal and informal permission-seeking. The formal steps for launching a Bible class may include receiving approval from the Christian Education Committee and the Church Council. If the plan has financial implications or requires refurnishing a room, then the steps involve the Finance Committee or the Trustees. Informal steps for launching the class may include receiving the approval of the pastor, cooperation from the church secretary, and the expectation that someone visits with existing Bible classes to see if they have any objection.

Some aspects of your church's system are visible and agreed upon. Other steps remain unseen and unspoken; they reflect expectations no one records, articulates, or maps out. It's the unknown, unstated, behind-the-scenes aspects of the system that mystify people who are new to the church. A system can seem completely impenetrable to newcomers.

The following are some of the ways our systems say *No*:

The Church with a Thousand Steps. *A thousand steps* doesn't refer to a dramatic architectural feature leading up from the sidewalk to the sanctuary doors but to the inordinately difficult, multiphased way the church makes its decisions.

If you were to trace how an idea moves through your church's system from initial inspiration to ultimate fruition, you might be surprised. Some congregations require not one, two, or three steps but as many as seven or eight. The simplest proposal is discussed multiple times over several months in numerous settings with many of the same people present at every step.

People who champion a ministry never know where they stand or whether the idea will make it. Everyone encourages them, but nothing gets done.

The Church That Can't Decide. According to Jim Collins, author of *Good to Great*, a distinctive quality of nonprofits is the way authority is distributed in such a diffuse way across the entire organization.[1] Within churches, authority rests in varying degrees with the pastor, staff, elected leadership, committees, councils, various small groups, "tribal leaders" who wield significant influence because of the long-standing respect others afford them, and a host of other constituencies, including women's groups, men's organizations, adult classes, the choir, the day school, and so forth. Because of the diffuse nature of church organizations, no one can give final approval to any project even though anyone can veto it or slow it down. Anyone can stop progress, but no one has the authority to say *Yes* so the project gets done.

The pastor and lay leadership do not administer operations from atop a structured and disciplined hierarchy like the CEO of a business might. In fact, leaders can only exercise their authority by the power of persuasion and by an appeal to common values. They lead an all-volunteer army.

For instance, the pastor, the trustees, and the council may agree that the church needs to remodel the parlor. But if the class of elderly adults who meet each Sunday in the parlor resists the change, their informal "vote" may carry more weight than the combined approval of the elected leaders.

Leaders find they have less authority than they thought when faced with a difficult personnel issue, such as an oppositional music director or ineffective church secretary who nevertheless remains popular with members.

Most churches don't have enough executive authority concentrated in one role or committee to act. This results in convoluted systems that seek and re-seek approval from numerous groups until finally everyone agrees, or until the idea loses steam and fades away.

Pastors and committee chairs often appear less decisive, less focused, and more reserved in exercising authority than business leaders in similar-sized companies.[2] In the business world, the executive leader has enough concentrated power to simply make decisions. In diffuse nonprofit organizations, no one—including the pastor—has enough structural power to make things happen.

In a diffuse organization, everyone believes that things should change, but no one can make it happen. Leaders can't select the people they need, and they have difficulty removing people who are ineffective. It's nearly impossible to eliminate unsuccessful programs, even when everyone knows they're not working.

People feel frustrated when congregations officially laud the generation of new ideas while simultaneously subverting the implementation of those same ideas through systems that restrain and limit and delay.

The Church That Takes Forever. Several youth suggested that a church should build a sand volleyball court to attract young people from the neighborhood. The youth took the idea to the youth director, and she took it to a staff meeting, where the idea was discussed several times. Eventually, the pastor carried the suggestion to the trustees. The trustees approved, and handed it over to the finance committee. The finance committee presented it to the church council. The council set up a task force with representatives from the youth, staff, finance committee, and trustees. The task force researched the idea and brought a proposal back to the church council who discussed it and sent it back to the finance committee to develop a plan to pay for it. The finance committee sent cost estimates to the youth council so that they could work on fundraising. The money was raised, and the plan went back to the council to receive final approval.

When the contractor began excavation, he discovered a drainage issue, and suggested a different location on church property. The trustees decided to move the volleyball court, but needed approval from the staff, youth, and church council for the change.

The entire process took eighteen months!

A sand volleyball court affects money, property, and ministry. It involves excavation, drainage, aesthetics, maintenance, and long-term costs. The many steps actually seem logical, and we can see why each step was taken in the order it was taken.

When we step back to look at the system from a distance, we realize the maze of steps and the incredible slowness of the decision, even though everyone supported the idea. The dizzying number of meetings took forever. Some of the youth who were in high school when the idea emerged were halfway through college by the time it was completed!

Many churches have just as elaborate a maze for far simpler decisions that have no effect on the budget. Painting the nursery, hiring a part-time musician, forming a Volunteers in Mission team, or starting a Sunday school class follow just as circuitous and lengthy a process.

Long-time leaders expect slow, complex systems, but newcomers are amazed and frustrated. People give up and withdraw when the system takes forever.

The Church of a Thousand Rules. Gordon MacKenzie has written a delightful book on organizations titled *Orbiting the Giant Hairball.*[3] The *hairball* is MacKenzie's term for the accumulated procedures and policies that get set in stone in an organization. The "hairs" of the hairball begin as good ideas and practices that initially solve a problem. They then get codified into rules that everyone has to follow. These rules accumulate far beyond their usefulness. Every new policy is another hair for the hairball, and hairs are never taken away, only added. The hairball grows enormous until it has its own heavy mass and gravity that pulls everything into the tangled web of established rules, policies, procedures, standards, and systems. The hairball stifles creativity, makes change nearly impossible, robs people of spirit, limits innovation, slows response, and restrains initiative. Even small organizations develop large, complex hairballs over the course of decades.

Have you experienced a church that is stuck in place by its own collection of rules and procedures? Church meetings often result in enlarging the hairball rather than in encouraging greater ministry. Committees spend endless hours refining policies, tightening rules, or arguing over their application.

The tendency toward complexity begins at the denominational level. The United Methodist *Book of Discipline*, for instance, grows in size and complexity with each General Conference, incorporating more paragraphs that begin, "The congregation shall . . . the pastor shall . . . the lay leader shall . . . the trustees shall." This limits flexibility and contextual creativity. There are 4,835 "shalls" in the *Book of Discipline*! Thousands of paragraphs require, direct, and limit the actions of committees, boards, and councils. The congregation adds more mandates and policies of their own.

Obviously, we need order for our operational essentials, but do we expand the mission of the church each time we establish a new policy and create a new committee? A tight tapestry of interlocking rules becomes impenetrable. The system becomes so unfriendly for users that people give up.

The Report, Review, Rehash, and Redo Church. A young dental hygienist shared with me her excitement about being invited by her church to serve on their primary governance council. She was honored and humbled by the invitation to serve in a decision-making role.

After her first meeting, I asked her how things went. She rolled her eyes, shook her head, and then described the most boring and purposeless meeting she had ever attended. Some people droned on and on about every little topic. They heard reports from every possible person, group, and ministry. "It was excruciating. I felt like my ears were bleeding!" she said. No decisions were made and no action was taken. It was a waste of her time.

Many congregational governance systems are not equipped to focus leadership on the primary purpose of the church. Committees meet because they are required to rather than to identify priorities or to take meaningful action. Most meetings simply don't matter and follow a pattern of reporting rather than of learning, discussing, or decision making that improves ministries. Committee members can't see the connection between the use of their time and the mission of the church. As one lay member said, "We report, review, rehash, and redo the same work that staff and committees have already done."

Such a system discourages and restrains. Nothing new takes root.

The Church of Micromanagers. While working with a larger congregation, I found myself wondering why such a talented staff and gifted leaders seemed unable to clarify purpose, identify priorities, and make decisions that fostered greater ministry. Why were they stuck?

The council met every month for two hours or more. The finance committee, trustees, and several other ministry teams also met monthly for lengthy sessions. I could not imagine why they needed so many meetings to accomplish so little.

When I reviewed the minutes of the council meetings, I discovered that members spent endless amounts of time discussing whether a Bible study should start at six or six-thirty, whether it should meet on Tuesday or on Thursday, and whether it should meet upstairs or in the parlor. Every detail of every ministry was discussed in excruciating detail. Similarly, the finance committee discussed each expenditure on every line item in the budget, and trustees deliberated on every individual request for the use of the building. Leaders were drowning in details.

Agendas so full of minutia leave little room for conversations about purpose, priority, mission, and innovation. The system crowds out new ideas and the people who present them.

The Up-or-Down Church. The Up-or-Down church makes decisions without considering multiple options and weighing various alternatives. The church decides "whether or not" on one alternative and focuses on one option rather than a spectrum of approaches. The Up-or-Down church never searches for a middle way or for a means to take the first steps, because every vote is all or nothing, yes or no, now or never, up or down. Bold projects that require research, training, or experimentation never receive enough permission to try.

The Church That Focuses on How Too Soon. As well as forcing an up or down vote, many churches also fall into the trap of asking *how* too soon.[4] How much? How long? How many? How will you deal with this or that? When asked too early in the creative process, these reasonable-sounding questions are an expression of doubt and focus the conversation on obstacles rather than ends. *How* questions tilt the conversation too heavily too soon toward what is doable, practical, and known, and thereby reduce the scope of conversation to something much smaller than what would otherwise be possible. Immediately demanding answers to *How* questions limits projects prematurely or causes us to focus on approaches we are already familiar with. Creative conversations give more time earlier to intention, purpose, and mission. Too much focus too early on methodology causes us to avoid delving more deeply into what we really want to do, what needs to be done, or to the change God is really calling us to make.

Moses was called by God to set the Hebrew people free from their slavery in Egypt. He immediately interrupts God's calling with a number of *how* questions before the complete vision could be absorbed or understood. How will I get their attention, how will I get them to follow me, how will I change Pharaoh's mind, how will they find food, how am I going to speak to them. This huge, compelling, God-sized vision could have died right there. God could have said, "Yep, that's a problem. Let's put this off until we fix your speech and all those other things first."

The Church with an Unreasonable Number of Reasonable Questions. Many leaders believe their primary responsibility is to demand answers. Leaders should ask reasonable questions to determine that an idea aligns with the mission, matches congregational priorities. Good questions refine an idea.

But a premature and paralyzing demand for data kills a project. People who feel called to explore a ministry become discouraged when they confront too many questions too early, before they have had time to work through the possibilities. Too quick a confrontation with leaders who demand answers to everything can cause an idea to suffer death by a thousand questions.

Unhelpful Expectations

Congregations have a set of expectations, mostly unspoken and never completely identified, about the style of worship they prefer, the pastoral care they desire, the programs of the church they like, and the processes by which they make decisions. Imagine writing down all those expectations and drawing a circle around them.[5]

In effect, the congregation authorizes leaders to operate within that circle. So long as leaders meet those expectations, the congregation feels content and well-served. Pastors who figure out what people expect and do it will be rewarded. Likewise, laypersons who do what the pastor expects and fulfill assigned roles on committees are appreciated. However, if leaders merely focus on fulfilling existing expectations within that circle, the ministry grows inward-focused and the church stagnates by repeating the same ministries from year to year. Some expectations are unhelpful, limiting, or result in systems that paralyze and restrain.

Leaders must move beyond the expectations of current long-standing members, operate outside the comfort zone of the congregation, and try new things in order to reach people with different expectations.

Several unhelpful expectations drive systems toward complexity and intransigence.

Everyone Has to Know Everything
The first unhelpful expectation is the belief that everyone needs to know everything, and the church can't act until everyone approves.

This expectation causes us to circulate ideas through an endless number of committees up and down the organizational chart. It slows down processes and requires people to vote and re-vote on mundane decisions.

Many leaders expect to be included in every decision. "Why wasn't I asked about that? Why didn't that come through my committee?" Leaders genuinely search for clarity about their responsibilities. Yet when every leader expects to be included, the system becomes increasingly complex. No one wants to be left out of the loop.

The expectation that everyone has to know everything both reveals and fosters lower trust. If laity do not trust staff, the finance committee has no confidence in the mission team, the council questions the motivations of the day school, and old-timers mistrust newcomers, then the church creates a system overpowered by rules, prescribed procedures, slow processes, and long circular sequences of permission seeking.

Changing this expectation requires a conscious decision, and it demands a higher level of trust and maturity. It requires leaders who can let go when it's appropriate to let go.

As one long-time layperson told me, "Sometimes I have to let go in order for someone else to take hold."

Growing churches reach a point where no one person knows everything that's going on. The insistence that someone, or everyone, must know everything limits growth.

Moreover, the expectation that everyone must know and approve gives tremendous power to discontented members. The whole church can be held hostage by a few people who object. Regrettably, meeting everyone's expectations slows down processes and expands the size and number of committees. The desire to please everyone is a prescription for decline. Leaders must be able to handle the stress of occasionally disappointing people.

When Pastor Janelle starts a worship service and Dana forms a disaster response team, they step beyond the expectations of existing members in response to a calling they care passionately about. Stepping beyond the circle of current expectations is a risky place to go. Rather than feeling rewarded for following their callings to offer a new ministry, they experience both personal and systemic resistance by leading their churches beyond the normal expectations, doing something that the church has not asked them, authorized them, or expected them to do.

Pastor Janelle with her desire to launch an alternative worship service and Dana with her interest in forming a disaster response ministry are dancing on the edge of their authority.[6] They are exercising leadership rather than merely fulfilling expectations. They are mobilizing people to meet a challenge consistent with the mission of the church and to offer ministry that will change the lives of hundreds of people. Yet, they are knowingly disappointing expectations at a pace they hope their members can absorb.[7]

John Wesley and other church reformers, the Apostle Paul and other early church leaders all danced on the edge of their authority. They met enough of the existing expectations to operate with authority and stay connected with the community while also following God's call to move beyond what was expected.

Churches that expect that everyone must approve everything surrender at the first sign of disagreement. They coddle critics and modify plans to appease anyone who objects. They settle for mediocrity instead of demanding excellence and fruitfulness. They accept a peaceful intransigence and a less-threatening inertia rather than pushing for action.

All Risk Must Be Avoided

A second unhelpful expectation is that all risk should be avoided. Congregations with overly complex systems expect that the role of leadership is to eliminate risk and prevent mistakes. The committees through which an idea must pass for approval serve as checks and balances. Congregations withhold permission out of sense of fear—fear of failure, fear of wasting money, fear of criticism, and even fear of success.

The protection of the church should rightly weigh on the minds of those who hold responsibility for leadership. But our complex and convoluted systems have less to do with avoiding catastrophe and more to do with avoiding criticism. The extraordinarily cautious quality of our systems makes it difficult to say *Yes*. In an attempt to reduce risks and avoid criticism, we enlarge and complicate the loop through which new ideas must travel until we develop systems so paralyzed that nothing happens. Doing nothing is less anxiety producing that doing something that might not work.

Growing churches overcome the risk-averse nature of most congregations. They give permission to experiment. They tolerate greater uncertainty.

Our hardest work may have little visible impact, or may end in utter failure. Sometimes alcoholics we help return to addictions, homes we build are destroyed by the next flood, and ex-cons we encourage end up back in prison. Ministry is risky.

In the parable Jesus tells about the sower, some seeds land on rocky ground, get choked by weeds or gobbled by birds. Likewise, many of our finest efforts never result in visible fruit. But as the parable promises, when we remain faithful to the task, a harvest comes forth in miraculous ways. Christ's ministry requires our willingness to risk failure.

To move from systems that control to systems that encourage, leaders have to become more comfortable with risk. Wise leaders say *Yes* even knowing the idea may not work or that someone will criticize the decision.

Leadership Means Control

A third unhelpful expectation that leads churches to create convoluted permission-seeking systems is that leadership means control rather than getting things done.

Thomas Friedman compares countries that have lengthy, complicated, and expensive requirements for starting companies with countries that have quicker, simpler, and less costly requirements. In some countries, you can start a company in two weeks with little paperwork, nominal regulation, and few fees. In other countries, it takes eighteen months to start a business, requires compliance with countless regulations, and demands payment for expensive permits.[8]

Which countries are thriving in the global economy? Those with simpler, quicker, and less costly permission-granting processes. Friedman suggests that everywhere that you see unnecessarily complex processes for starting a business, you find greater corruption and protection of prerogative.

I'm not suggesting church leaders are corrupt! But our complex systems do protect the prerogatives of those in control.

Churches that believe leadership means control refuse new people a place at the table. They make entry into the church and its leadership lengthy, complicated, and difficult. They perceive newcomers as threats, as irresponsible, and as disrupters. They re-elect the same people year after year. They resist change, growth, restructuring, or streamlining. They treat newcomers as outsiders. They prefer doing things the way they've always done them before. By so doing, leaders protect their prerogative, defend their territory, and retain a measure of control. They behave as if the governing board is a group elected and set apart to tell people what they cannot do.

I recall a church treasurer who exerted extraordinary control. When someone offered a proposal that the treasurer didn't support, he'd check the books, shake his head, and tell everyone that there was no money in the budget. He'd describe all the steps involved in amending the budget and how long it would take. In a multimillion-dollar budget, he could never find $100 for something he didn't support.

When the treasurer liked an idea, his attitude changed. He'd find a dozen places in the budget with unspent balances, and would suggest we shift money from those. Amending the budget became quick and easy. He could find thousands of dollars if the project was one he approved. The treasurer was a good person, but he wielded extraordinary control on the system and protected his prerogative to do so by his specialized knowledge of the finances.

In another church, the pastor exerted a similar control. Every decision required his approval. He squelched any dream that wasn't his own. People expected that the pastor was the only one who could bring new ideas and lead the resulting ministries. The downward pressure on the energy of laypersons was palpable, creating members who were followers rather than leaders.

Leadership does not mean control; it means getting things done. Leaders help organizations fulfill their mission. They address challenges that constrain. Leaders mobilize people. They empower rather than limit, multiply rather than restrain, encourage rather than discourage. They help the church fulfill its mission by helping people fulfill their callings.

When people confuse leadership with control, they expend an extraordinary amount of time and energy restricting other people from doing ministry!

Meetings Are Where the Action Is

Congregations with complex governance systems operate with a fourth unhelpful expectation, that meetings are where the action is.

I once compared the calendar of events printed on the back of the Sunday bulletin from a church in decline with the weekly calendar of the same church several years later after it had reversed direction and experienced significant growth. The earlier calendar listed one Sunday service, an evening youth meeting, a weekly choir rehearsal, and no other ministries. However, nearly every weekday night included one or more of the following meetings: the finance committee, the trustees, the nominations committee, the administrative board, the council on ministries, or committees for property, personnel, Christian education, missions, or worship.

Several years later, after the church reversed its decline and began to grow, the weekly calendar included four worship services, more than a dozen adult Bible studies, numerous ministries for children and youth, a variety of volunteer opportunities for people to work in the schools and community, and several support groups related to various addictions, family situations, and health issues plus numerous rehearsals for music teams and choirs. There were fellowship dinners and prayer teams and women's ministries and men's retreats. There were weekend seminars, mission projects, softball games, and fundraisers. The calendar filled two pages. Nowhere on the calendar could I find any administrative meetings scheduled!

If you were drawn to this congregation twenty years ago, felt a desire to belong and to participate, how would you have perceived what was important based on that earlier calendar? The calendar answers such questions as, "Where's the action in this church? What's the most significant activity? How do I do my part?" You would have thought, "I'd like to serve on the trustees or the finance committee someday. If I earn people's respect, maybe they'll ask me to serve on the church council."

Today, the calendar would say something different about what's most important and how you might serve. The church expects that you would grow in your sense of belonging by joining a Bible study, serving on a mission team, or singing in a praise band. Mentors encourage you to deepen your ministry rather than to serve on a committee. With time and experience, you might be called upon to teach a Bible class, lead a mission team, start a support group, sing in the praise band, or help with a worship service.

The underlying expectation twenty years ago was that meetings are where the action is. Today, ministry is where the action is. The focus now is less on running the church and more on serving in ministry, and there are more spiritually engaged laypersons and fewer people serving on committees.

The congregation still has an infrastructure, governance, and committees. It has policies and strategies and budgets. Laypersons are still elected to serve, but these teams are mostly behind-the-scenes. They are support structures for ministry, like the bones of the body—essential, but operating unseen. More importantly, the church operates with a clear mission statement, a vision, and a common set of values.

The critical question "Which committee would you like to serve on?" has changed to "What ministry do you see God calling you to fulfill?" Top-down, highly structured churches predetermine how people can serve rather than form ministries that are grown out of a sense of calling and serve the present context.

The goal of traditional structures is to help leaders manage, control, and coordinate ministries that already exist. Such structures are far less effective for giving birth to and supporting new ministries.

One church had photos on the wall of a men's Bible class from the 1950s that showed more than four hundred people in attendance. The congregation in that era had hundreds of children in Sunday school and hundreds of women in the denominational women's organization that worked for mission causes. The uniform structures and committees prescribed by the denomination helped coordinate these existing ministries with consistency from congregation to congregation.

That world no longer exists. Now the task is how to start a men's study, how to launch a Wednesday evening children's ministry, and how to initiate a successful weekend retreat for women.

Churches with more meetings than ministry become inward-centered rather than outward-focused. They put more energy into structure than into serving. They become obsessed with maintaining the infrastructure rather than fostering ministry.

Why It Matters

Why take the time to reexamine our systems? Does it matter how many steps it takes to make decisions or initiate ministries?

A Fading Relevance

When churches work with antiquated and confusing systems, their method of operation becomes less relevant and more distant from real-world needs. Approaching outdated systems is like stepping into a time machine taking us to a previous age of complex bureaucracies, obscure rules, quaint traditions, endless reports, and infinitely slow processes.

Outsiders perceive what we do as irrelevant to their lives and to the needs of the world. This crisis of relevance is especially true for next generations. Young people wonder how present-day congregations, with their facilities and budgets and meetings, have any demonstrable bearing on the mission of Christ. So much of the activity seems pointless, or at least extraneous, to the sufferings of the world or to the capacity of congregations to help.

The focus on internal mechanisms draws attention inward and away from the mission field. An endless entanglement of rules and redundant steps for approval are avoidance behaviors, keeping us from addressing the harder questions about who we are, what we do, and why it matters.

As David Kinnaman and Gabe Lyons have described in *UnChristian*, younger generations view Christians in general as judgmental, anti-homosexual, hypocritical, old-fashioned, too political, out of touch with reality, insensitive to others, and boring.[9] Young people perceive our reliance on meetings and our internal squabbles as unattractive and as impediments to serving. They view these methods as unapproachable, confusing, and ineffective.

A fading relevance is also seen in the growing distance between the people in the pew and the leaders of the church. The issues that matter most to the everyday Christian seeking to grow in grace and searching for channels to serve are not the same things that fill the agendas of our meetings. Endless reports, long meetings, and lengthy policies leave people blurry-eyed rather than highly motivated.

Laypersons who perceive congregational structures as restraining influences that draw their attention away from their calling become more selective about what they are willing to give their time to or agree to participate in. Churches desire a closer relationship to their members than members want with their churches.

Some younger people question the relevance of congregations altogether. They want to explore the spiritual life and feel called to make a difference in the world, but the meetings and committees seem like spinning wheels. They're not convinced that such activities relate to the mission of Christ.

More Immediate Options

In his book *The World Is Flat,* Thomas Friedman describes the ever-increasing disruption in institutions and corporations as people rely on instant communication and new forms of technology to establish relationships and partnerships directly without the help of corporate or governmental channels. People can contact other people directly, personally, and immediately through mobile phones, the Internet, and Facebook. Anyone can access anything anytime from anywhere to find what they want and connect with other people with similar interests. This has changed the world for journalists, retailers, music producers, banks, and universities.[10]

People don't need institutions for many of the essential services that institutions used to provide. Neither do people need to go through an institution to fulfill their calling to serve.

Disintermediation means the elimination of intermediaries. For instance, people don't need a bookstore between them and their books, and so they order online. People don't need a publisher between them and their favorite writers, and so self-publishing has emerged. People don't need a physical book between them and the ideas of the authors they like, and so we have e-books.

Similarly, people don't need a downtown bank building between them and their checking accounts, and so we have branch banking. Nor do they need any bank building between them and their money, and so we have on-line banking. People don't need a television network between them and their entertainment nor newspapers between them and their news. Every aspect of life, culture, and business has been affected by the forces of disintermediation, and that's what Friedman means when he says the world is flat. You don't have to go through an institution to get things done.

This new world also shapes how people relate to congregations and creates a new world of options for people who desire to serve Christ. People today have access to spiritual resources from a variety of places, and it's not uncommon for an active layperson to attend worship at the church where they belong, participate in retreats with another church, and serve on work projects with another. Laypersons rely upon denominational curriculum for some small groups while also utilizing a variety of books, blogs, videos, and podcasts on faith and spirituality.

In the example that opens this chapter, Dana feels called to respond to the suffering of people in a community devastated by a tornado. In former times, the only option she had for helping people in another state was through her denomination or church. She relied entirely upon the institution of the church to provide a channel to help, through personal donations, preparing medical kits, gathering food supplies, or organizing a work team. She waited for the denomination or the congregation to act, and then joined in to do her part.

In the flat world of social media and the Internet, Dana immediately has countless other options for making a difference. Dozens of relief organizations provide her with channels to donate money, some of them more trustworthy than others. Countless organizations solicit volunteers or lead drives to collect clothing.

Dana doesn't have to wait for her church to act. If the systems at the church are too slow, too complicated, or too difficult to engage, she can fulfill her calling by turning to another organization or another church.

Today, systems for connecting and serving are direct, personal, immediate. This has huge implications for congregations that rely upon centralized control, multiple steps, and lengthy processes. People no longer tolerate the complexity and slowness. In the world young people live in, many things happen at once with extraordinary immediacy. They expect quick responses, agility, and rapid action. Rather than waiting until the next meeting, young adults e-mail, text, compose, and research a proposed action while the current meeting is going on. No shortage of altruistic impulses exists among young adults today, but many of them choose more accessible channels to express their callings.

Church leaders who give their best in systems that do not acknowledge the flat world find their work increasingly difficult and less relevant. Maintaining and enforcing slow, complex, multistep, centralized systems takes extraordinary energy in a flat world, and working harder to keep them going reaps fewer and fewer benefits. We struggle against this new world as something foreign, or we embrace it for the mission of the church.

Nothing Gets Done

When our systems say *No*, nothing gets done. We fail to fulfill the fundamental mission given us in Christ. Ministry diminishes. Members become more passive and less engaged. They surrender to the status quo. We filter out too many good ideas, and our most creative, talented, and passionate people give up. The callings of our laypersons are ignored, denied, or thwarted. The church gets stuck, and simply repeats the same ministries it offers every year, getting the same results—growing a little smaller, older, and more inward focused.

We can do better.

Questions for Reflection and Discussion

1. "Many congregations require five to seven layers of organizational approval, and each person or committee has the ability to say *No*, but nobody has the authority to say *Yes*." How have you experienced this dynamic in your congregation?

2. How does the notion of an organizational *hairball*, an accumulated set of policies and procedures that slow change and restrain innovation, help you understand some of your experiences in church leadership? How have your decisions contributed to the *hairball*?

3. When was a time that something could not get done because no one had authority to act, even though everyone thought it was the right thing to do?

4. Can you think of a time when you navigated organizational restraints to offer fresh and innovative ministry? How did you do it?

5. How does your congregation avoid becoming a *Report, Review, Rehash, and Redo Church*? Or a *Church of Micromanagers*?

6. The chapter names several unhelpful expectations, including *Everyone Has to Know Everything, All Risk Must Be Avoided, Leadership Means Control*, and *Meetings Are Where the Action Is*. How have one or more of these expectations shaped your own response to new ideas?

To Delve Deeper

Read some of the passages where Jesus confronts the corrupting influence of systems more tied to their rules than to God-inspired purposes. For a fresh look at Matthew 23, read it in Eugene Peterson's translation, *The Message*, and notice the lines about becoming roadblocks to God's kingdom and the bundles of rules loading people down like pack animals! Or if that's too harsh, read Luke 6:1-11 in *The Message*.

Prayer

Reach down to where we are, Lord, and untangle us from our own rules. Help us flourish in our following of your way. Grant us patience and perseverance as we practice your love so that things we formerly thought were impossible become real in our community of faith and in our ministry to others.

Chapter Three

Buildings, Bulletins, and Attitudes

Churches That Say *No*

Why have people come to expect that the answer to anything new in the church is *No*? Perhaps it's because the church sends a thousand subtle messages of being closed to new people, new ideas, and new experiences without even realizing it. Not only are some churches saying *No* to new ideas, they are saying *No* to new people without being aware they are doing so.

You're Welcome Here, But...

When their children reached school age, Cynthia and Kevin decided the time was right to explore faith and experience worship as a family. This marked a return to church for Kevin, but Cynthia had grown up without any religious experience. Both valued spirituality but viewed organized religion with suspicion.

Their first weeks attending worship were awkward, but they were attracted by the preaching, found the music appealing, and appreciated the general friendliness of the people. Welcome signs adorned the foyer, greeters eagerly handed them brochures, and everyone was cordial. Yet, they couldn't help but notice subtle behaviors that seemed to undermine the atmosphere of hospitality. For example, even after several weeks, people continued to refer to them as visitors. No one learned their names, and they reintroduced themselves to the same greeters and staff members week after week. They became uncomfortable by disapproving glances whenever their children made noise during worship. They responded to an appeal for volunteers by signing up in the foyer but never were contacted. They attended a Bible class for people their age, and while everyone was polite, no one engaged them in conversation.

They attended a church dinner but ended up sitting by themselves. They even met with the pastor and formally joined the church but still they felt like outsiders. No one expressed interest in them or their children, and with their attempts to engage seemingly rejected, they felt like the kids in grade school who were the last selected for the team. The final straw was when one of their children was scolded for innocently bringing a drink into a room that had a rule that prohibited beverages. Looking back, Cynthia says, "It felt like no one cared whether we were there or not. We wondered if this was because we were younger than most of the members, or because we didn't grow up in the community, or because one of our children was of a different ethnic background. It took so much energy to engage people that we eventually drifted away." Ultimately, they began searching for another church.

Every explicit comment said *Yes*, but somehow Cynthia and Kevin felt they were pushing against a subtle, but powerful, *No*.

Cynthia's and Kevin's experience is more common than we realize. Newcomers visit five or six times, then fade away. The fact that they return for several weeks indicates they find something meaningful and engaging. Perhaps the sermon or music or outward friendliness appeals to them. That they drift away means the church is not connecting with them.

Too many churches want more young people so long as they act like old people, more newcomers as long as they act like old-timers, more children as long as they are as quiet as adults, more ethnic families as long as they act like the majority in the congregation.

Saying *No* Without Realizing It

The church that Cynthia and Kevin joined thinks of itself as a welcoming congregation, open to change and to new ideas. Instead, outsiders and newcomers feel closed out and shut down. The church thinks it's saying *Yes*, when in fact it is saying *No*. The following are some of the ways churches say *No* without even realizing it:

Visitors Feel Uncomfortable. One way of saying *No* without knowing it is through behaviors that make new people feel uncomfortable. Reminding visitors that they are sitting in your favorite pew, asking them to wear nametags when regular attendees don't, making them stand up in worship to introduce themselves—these focus a spotlight on visitors that most find intrusive and awkward. Whispering about visitors rather than speaking with them, sending disapproving signals about the behavior of their children, or ignoring them altogether as if they don't exist—these activities are as rude and unwelcoming in church as they would be anywhere. Visitors already feel self-conscious about being new, and they do not want to be made to feel even more conspicuous.

Insider Language and Secret Codes. Another means by which a congregation signals *No* to newcomers is by using insider language and acronyms in bulletins, flyers, and announcements: "The Rebecca Circle will meet at Ann Wilson's home on Tuesday," "Sign Up for VBS," "UMM Breakfast on Saturday Morning," "Alpha and Omega Registration Open," "Kairos Needs Your Help."

These make perfect sense to long-time members, but they sound like a foreign language to newcomers. They are inscrutable unless you know the code, such as what a "Circle" is and where the Wilsons live, that VBS means Vacation Bible School, and UMM means United Methodist Men, and that Alpha and Omega is a Bible class, and Kairos is a service ministry.

As people gathered for worship at one congregation, the prelude began and the following announcements appeared on the projection screens: "The Worship Committee meeting for Tuesday has been postponed," "There will be no chancel choir rehearsal this Wednesday," "The Missions Office will be closed until July 15," "The Youth Fellowship does not meet until August," "Staff Meeting on Tuesday morning at 10 a.m."

No welcome. No positive announcements. No events or ministries. No opportunities to get involved. The announcements were merely a litany of events that have been cancelled, postponed, closed, or which pertained to only a select group of people. What is a visitor to think?

Churches attuned to creating an invitational atmosphere never conduct insider business during a worship service meant for visitors; they should only announce events that apply to everyone.

No Follow-Through. A family new to the community visited worship services at several churches, and they signed the registration pad at the churches that interested them, requesting more information. No one contacted them or sent information. However, one church surprised them by delivering a small gift and a package of information, even though they had completed no forms and requested no information. Their experience reminded them of the story Jesus tells about a father who requested that his sons go work in the vineyard. One said *No*, but changed his mind and went to work, while the other said *Yes*, but then never followed through. "Which one of these two did his father's will?" Jesus asks (Matt 21:31). The family joined the church that exceeded expectations.

Churches sometimes send out inventories asking people to identify projects they would like to volunteer for or post sign-up sheets for volunteers.

Some churches complete a lengthy inventory of the interests, gifts, and passions of members. When people give their name, phone number, and e-mail address on a sign-up sheet, they expect someone will contact them. The church is saying *Yes*, we value your gifts and we want you to serve. But if no one follows up and the members never hear another word or the inventories are neglected, the church has said *No* by its inability or unwillingness to follow through.

The Middle Doors. A mid-sized congregation noticed that while they received many new visitors, and a high percentage of them were joining, nevertheless attendance remained steady month after month. Why was attendance leveling off? The church practiced hospitality with excellence, with visitors and new members feeling welcomed at worship. But then after a few months, visitors and new members would become less consistent in attendance and then discontinue altogether. To better understand, the pastor visited with some members who had recently joined.

The pastor discovered that people felt welcomed and supported when they first visited the church and continued to feel a sense of belonging in worship. But when they tried to become part of Sunday school classes, men's organizations, choirs, and Bible studies, they found the groups cliquish, uninterested in welcoming new people. Even after months of trying, they felt at the margins in these smaller groups and ministries. One woman said, "Before I moved here, I was the lead usher in my old church. I didn't expect to do that again here, but I hoped to join in somehow. When I showed up to help, everyone talked only to the people they already knew, and I felt invisible. I stood by myself. Insider jokes left me feeling isolated. I felt like they didn't need me or want me."

"The front door" was working well, as people felt invited and welcomed. But they were slipping out "the back door" because they were discovering too many of "the middle doors" were closed tight. The church was saying *Yes* to visitors in worship while saying *No* in small groups.

Leaders began a series of teaching events in the adult classes, mission teams, service organizations, choirs, and Bible studies to move the culture of hospitality deeper into the life of the church. As the small groups of the church began to grow, the worship attendance began to increase. New members seldom feel they belong to the church until they find meaningful connections in small groups beyond worship, and so churches must open the middle doors.

Underutilizing People. Sarah moved into the community and joined the church after retiring as vice-president of a mid-sized corporation. She had enjoyed a long history of engagement with community service projects and leadership in her previous church, and had served on the school board for a decade. In her mid-fifties, she now wanted to dedicate herself to service and ministry, and so she offered to volunteer in her new church in any way that was helpful.

She was invited to help with the team working on a church-wide dinner. She arrived early, was handed a package of napkins, and asked to distribute them at all the place settings. When she finished, she returned to the kitchen to discover that most of the other work was already being done. She found herself on the outside looking in at a tight-knit group of friends. She felt out of place, as no effort was made to include her.

After offering again to help, Sarah was invited to a Saturday work day to clean out a closet of old children's ministry materials. A week later, the secretary phoned to ask her help for folding newsletters.

These simple tasks were fine with Sarah; she was not averse to helping in any way. But her yearning to make a difference by using her talents in retirement was not going to be fulfilled through her church. Her executive experience, community service, insight into organizations, and ability to mobilize people were gifts the church seemed unable or unprepared to use. Except for attending worship, she drifted away from active involvement and searched for community organizations that could channel her impulses to make a positive difference in the lives of people.

When churches underutilize people, they dampen the callings and spiritual aspirations of volunteers. Many laity yearn to make a difference and want to express their faith through ministries that change lives, but the church doesn't know how to use their gifts.

Churches that provide no channels for service that are intellectually stimulating, spiritually renewing, and life-changing limit members to an entry-level faith with little hope of maturing or advancing in discipleship. Volunteer service that only involves simple tasks and mundane work doesn't support the development of courage, service, love, and sacrifice. Under these circumstances, members never feel competent or effective in living out their faith.

Many followers of Christ help with small projects at the church occasionally because that's the only opportunity the church provides. They set up tables, direct parking, put canned goods in boxes, or paint the youth room. They tutor children for a few weeks, and then later they're asked to deliver lunches to teams building wheelchair ramps for disabled persons. Each of these projects is good and worthy work. Yet the serving opportunities are sporadic, infrequent, and inconsistent. Volunteers dabble in doing good rather than fulfilling a calling that uses their best and highest gifts. Without focus, consistency, and persistence, volunteers feel frustrated, awkward, and ineffective. They're like students signing up for one tennis lesson, one piano lesson, one dance lesson, and one swimming lesson: when they look back, they wonder why they've never mastered any of them. They never learn and grow and mature in the art of serving.

Many volunteers are fine with light chores and simple tasks, and the church couldn't fulfill its mission without considerable numbers of people helping in such ways. But others are searching for a deeper commitment and wider experience that uses more of their time and talent. They have capacities for bold, significant, and complex ministries, but the church is unable to absorb, channel, or use their gifts.

We Don't Need You. In one church, members and guests were asked to bring canned goods each week in November to contribute to Thanksgiving baskets, which the church would deliver to families in need. Dozens of large boxes were filled, and a huge shipment of turkeys had been donated. A few thousand dollars had been raised to purchase fruits and vegetables to accompany the canned goods. An announcement was made recruiting people to volunteer to help sort, distribute, and deliver the baskets.

Alan and Amanda decided to help out along with their two elementary-aged children. They arrived on time to find several dozen people milling around. The food had already been gathered, the baskets had already been sorted, and the deliveries were already being made. The planning team had set things up the night before and then decided to work longer to get things going and had eventually completed the project before other volunteers ever arrived. The dozens of people who showed up to help were fed doughnuts and sent home.

Leaders sometimes invite people to help with a project but then do the work themselves before anyone else can help, leaving volunteers feeling like they've wasted their time. This happens with volunteer construction projects, clean up days, hanging of the greens, cooking teams, painting projects, clothes distribution, and rummage sales. People sign up to help, but two or three leaders do all the work before others have a chance. Leaders are saying *No* to the volunteer impulses of people when they leave them with nothing meaningful to do.

Blurry Messages. Week after week, the pastor preached sermons full of high rhetoric about the care for the poor, the concern for the oppressed, the fight for justice, the longing for community, and the love of all people. The sermons included admonitions to make disciples, heal the sick, serve the world. These high-sounding, noble generalizations were inevitably sprinkled with phrases like "you ought" and "you should" and "you must."

The sermons, however, lack specificity, clarity, originality, or practicality. Shallow platitudes, even those interspersed with scriptural references and communicated with sincerity, never give anyone direction on how to assimilate spiritual truths into daily life. While no one disagrees with the general themes, such blurry and unfocused messages lack any quality of incarnation. Generalized admonitions, divorced from specific context or tangible action, are heard as judgmental diatribes that leave people feeling beaten and without hope. Rather than encouraging, emboldening, and inviting people to greater ministry, the sermons leave listeners feeling unable to effect any change in themselves or the world. Rather than mobilizing people to act or inspiring them to think differently, platitudes neither connect nor motivate, and they diminish the impulse to act.

Conflict. A palpable sense of conflict between the pastor and the church leaders, within the staff, or among the laity can squeeze out new people and shut down any chance of new ideas emerging. Internal conflict takes attention away from what the church should be doing. Like a magnet beside a compass, conflict draws congregations off course.

Bickering, blaming, backbiting, and griping make participation and leadership uninviting. With conflict and mistrust, the church resorts to greater legalism through rules, controls, and steps for withholding permission. Persons who don't get along with one another make it difficult for everyone else to focus on the mission. Some churches get drawn into larger divisive issues, allowing differences about politics, social issues, or community challenges to sabotage the work of the church.

In a badly conflicted church, ministry is stymied by the attitude that "if it's your idea, I'm opposed to it." Initiatives get squeezed out by conflict, fear, reactivity, and control issues in the same way the seeds in the parable of the sower get strangled by weeds or gobbled by birds.

Conflicted churches attract people who thrive on conflict, and a self-reinforcing pattern begins with people struggling for control, insisting on their own way, and discounting anyone who disagrees.

Congregations that live with a constant sense of threat can't provide space for creative conversation and for the prayerful cultivation of new ministries. Fear of financial collapse, the threat of closing, the discovery of misconduct accusations—any of these can paralyze a church.

***Signs That Say* No.** A church changed the time of its worship services, and moved the pastor's office to the former high school Sunday school room. Two years after these changes, the sign in front still had the old worship schedule, and the sign on the pastor's office still described it as the youth room. The incident sounds quaint, and church members found the delay in updating signs amusing, like a family joke that several recounted with self-deprecating good humor. But they might as well have hung a sign that said, "For Insiders Only" on the front of the church and one in the hallway that said, "You're on your own. Good luck!" Nothing about the facility said, "Welcome. We want you to feel at home here."

Another church had an attractive modern playground, which they had surrounded with a six foot chain link fence with barbed wire on top that was enclosed by a locked gate with a sign that read "No Unauthorized Use." My children were young and learning to read, and even they found the contradiction striking. "That's not the way a church should act," my oldest told me.

Churches may have to regulate parking and provide for security, but often the tone, content, harshness, and frequency of their signage sends a negative message. One suburban congregation had more than a dozen negative restrictive signs: No Parking. Violators Will Be Towed. Church Use Only. Reserved for Staff. No Loitering. No Skateboards. Do Not Enter. No Unaccompanied Children. Keep Out. These signs, combined with the burglar bars on the windows and the steel doors with security alarm decals, created an atmosphere that screamed *No, No, No!* Some years later, all the signs are gone except for a pleasant reminder that the parking lot is for church use. The playground signs now welcome visitors in Spanish and English and invite guests to help keep the grounds clean. There is a covered bulletin board near the playground with flyers inviting families to worship. The doors are glass and the burglar bars are gone. The church has experienced no increase in vandalism, theft, or damage, but has seen an increase in neighborhood families participating in worship.

***Facilities That Say* No.** Occasionally, a church has a playground that is overgrown with weeds and crowded with broken equipment, rusty slides, and swing-sets with peeling paint. The congregation might as well put up a fifty-foot billboard that says, "We Haven't Seen a Child at this Church in Fifty Years; We Don't Expect to See Any in the Next Fifty Years; and If You Love Your Children, You'll Take Them Somewhere Else!" That's a lot of words on a billboard, but that's how big a sign a neglected playground is.

Most churches say they welcome people who use wheelchairs or walkers, but their buildings speak a different message: "Sure we welcome people with disabilities here...so long as they can climb up the stairs and slide into the pews just like everyone else!" We can do better.

Facilities speak a message about what church members think of themselves, how importantly they take our mission, how confidently they see the future. Our buildings tell the world what we think about children, senior citizens, persons with disabilities, and how we regard visitors. What message are we sending?

Solid doors that give no indication of whether you are entering a common hallway, the sanctuary, or a classroom are far less hospitable than glass doors or doors with windows. Mingling areas and waiting areas and foyers are more friendly than facilities that open immediately into classrooms or offices.

Most young adults work in newer buildings with modern lighting, contemporary colors and textures, and fire security systems that make them feel safe. They eat at restaurants and sleep in hotels and attend movies that meet high standards. They are accustomed to quality and cleanliness in restrooms, and they hold high expectations about the safety of the nursery and classrooms for their children. Many feel like they're traveling back in time when they visit a church and see the 1950s institutional green paint, the rusty pipes and cramped toilets in restrooms, the dim lights in hallways, the absence of smoke detectors, and no handicapped accessibility.

Facilities work against the witness of welcome when newcomers struggle to figure out unmarked hallways and convoluted staircases that insiders have grown accustomed to. It is easier to create a culture of hospitality, an atmosphere that says *Yes*, in a building that communicates welcome and speaks of optimism about the future.

Imagine a board of trustees that views their work as a ministry that assures that the facilities communicate an unmistakable sense of welcome and complete accessibility. The board members might say, "Our purpose is to assure that these facilities serve the highest purposes of ministry in Christ's name, and we dedicate ourselves to excellence as we make the buildings as useful, inviting, friendly, and open as we possibly can."

Such a board searches for new ways to make the church look fresh, appealing, inviting, easy to navigate, safe, clean, and attractive. They're unsettled with anything less than the best, and they take immediate action when they see messy restrooms, peeling paint, musky carpets, inadequate lighting, potholes in parking lots, inadequate sound systems, or playgrounds overgrown with weeds. They create an environment that says *Yes*.

A Shadow Mission

Congregations work with a stated or implied mission related to the ministry of Christ. Some adopt purpose statements that are widely known and frequently repeated, such as the following examples:

Connected with God, Growing in Faith, Serving with Love
Honoring God through Worship, Witness, and Service

To Build an Outwardly Focused Christian Community in the Life
  of Grace
Leading People to an Active Faith in Jesus Christ
Faith, Friendship, Fellowship, Followership, and Fruit
Helping People to Know, Love, and Serve God

A mission statement, an expression of common practices, or a logo can communicate priorities, reinforce identity, and provide focus. Mission statements give direction to staff and volunteers about what matters most.

However, many congregations operate with unspoken shadow missions that actually drive behaviors or limit alternatives more than the stated mission and adopted values. The logo uses missional language to motivate but leaders use maintenance language to make decisions.

For instance, everyone may agree that the congregation's purpose is to make disciples of Jesus Christ for the transformation of the world. In actual practice, one or more of the following shadow missions may guide decisions, operating as a subscript to every conversation. In effect, an unspoken shadow mission says that our purpose and priority is to fulfill the following:

Preserve the building.
Keep everyone happy.
Maintain the organ.
Protect the pastor.
Get rid of the pastor.
Never upset the secretary.
Don't offend the choir.
Never ask for money.
Protect the endowment.
Maintain a family feel.
Never increase the budget.
Avoid disagreement.
Focus on current members.
Survive at all costs.

Most of these shadow missions are driven by fear—fear of conflict, of upsetting someone, of financial catastrophe, of losing a facility, of changing a way of life. Under the threat of conflict, division, or financial stress, all energies are redirected to security and survival, leaving little space for creativity or initiative.

In one city, three mainline congregations were built on Main Street more than a hundred years ago. Like most downtown congregations, they all experienced decline over a fifty-year period. Fifteen years ago, one of the congregations developed a second site to offer a different worship style. It has attracted young families and thrived. Another of the congregations sold their downtown property and relocated to where the population was growing. This congregation expanded its outreached, grew exponentially, and became a multicultural congregation known for its outward focus and mission.

The third congregation struggled to maintain their facility, saw their average age increase while attendance slowly declined. A consultant met with leaders to discuss the church's future and helped leaders to distinguish their stated mission from their shadow mission. Members realized that for three generations, the unspoken dual shadow mission was "preserve the building at any cost" and "maintain traditional worship with no changes." The shadow mission had caused them to reject any serious attempts to consider additional worship services or alternative sites even when newcomers and younger members were requesting them.

A shadow mission may begin as an appropriate initiative that serves the mission of the church but then turns negative because of a lost sense of proportion. For instance, one congregation was determined to build a fellowship hall and gym to expand its ministry and accommodate more outreach. The initiative derived from their desire to serve youth. The congregation spent months building consensus, voting, and agreeing to plans, and then months more planning a capital funds campaign. People contributed for three years, but the church did not receive enough money to proceed. So they planned a second pledge campaign.

Years passed since the original plans were adopted, the church continued slowly to decline, many of the original contributors passed away, and the church experienced a change of pastors twice. Nevertheless, leaders pressed for the new building with a relentless passion. All energies were obsessively directed at completing the task, even though the project would smother the congregation in debt. Ten years from the original planning, the project was finished, leaving the congregation committed to several more years of payments.

Rather than energizing leaders and multiplying ministries, the completion of the fellowship hall and gym marked the beginning of what the current pastor calls "the doldrums." People were weary, staff members were burned-out, leaders backed away from further responsibilities, and volunteers lost their motivation. The congregation had been so focused on the tangible goal of completing the building that when they finally completed it, no one knew what to do next. Building the gym had become an end in itself, larger and more compelling than the mission of the church.

Everything had been done *so that* the gym would be built; long lost was the idea that the gym was planned *so that* the church could reach more people. If the energies of the church are poured into projects *so that* something other than the mission statement of the church is fulfilled, then the congregation may be driven by a shadow mission.[1]

The Cumulative Effect

What's the cumulative effect of *No*? Where does a culture of *No* take us?

Imagine a church that says *No* to allowing Alcoholics Anonymous to meet in their building because "we don't want strangers in our church," and *No* to sending members to training to lead a Bible study series because "we can figure out how to do it ourselves." They say *No* to hosting a basketball league for youth because "they're not our kids anyway," and *No* to starting a divorce recovery group because "that's so negative." The church says *No* to advertising because some members think "churches shouldn't do that sort of thing," *No* to starting another worship service because "we like the service we have," and *No* to sending a mission work team internationally because "only seven people signed up." Leaders say *No* to starting a Bible study that meets in a home because the pastor can't be present to lead it, and *No* to starting a praise band because the choir director doesn't like that style of music. The church says *No* to volunteers who want to tutor at-risk youth because it requires opening the building in the evenings, and *No* to the donor who offered to pay for screens in the sanctuary because "people aren't ready for that yet."

The same church says *No* to launching a second Christmas Eve service because the organist refuses to play at two services, *No* to a women's group that wants to use study material from another denomination, *No* to a father/son banquet because it's not sponsored by the official men's organization, and *No* to the idea of a Wednesday youth ministry because the volunteers for the Sunday youth fellowship fear it will compete. The church says *No* to buying property next door because doing so would require a capital funds campaign, and *No* to remodeling the youth building because "we don't have enough young people to make it worthwhile." Leaders say *No* to starting a bilingual Bible study because "we'd have to find a teacher who speaks Spanish," and *No* to the plan to refurbish the parlor to make it multi-use because of the objections of the Bible class that meets once a week. The church says *No* to a fall stewardship campaign to cultivate generosity because "we shouldn't focus on money," *No* to conducting a sermon series because it interferes with the lectionary, *No* to a church-wide study because buying books for every household costs too much, and *No* to having a Children's Time in worship because it's too disruptive.

A church that consistently says *No* teaches people to accept *No* as the default answer. People become passive. They stop suggesting ideas, and they keep their callings to themselves. They expect the church to say *No*.

I'm not suggesting that a church should accept all of the ideas listed above, or that all of these would thrive and bear fruit. But as Wayne Gretsky, the championship hockey player, said, "You miss one hundred percent of the shots you never take."

Where does a consistent pattern of *No* take us? There is no movement, no initiative, no stretching, no risking, no reaching out. Numerical growth in congregations today happens rarely, reluctantly, and only by accepting significant change, and so churches that say *No* diminish possibilities for future ministry. The only people who remain are those satisfied with things exactly as they are. The path to ministry grows narrower and narrower. With each decade the average age of the members increases by six or seven years while attendance falls by 5 or 10 percent until no one is left but a handful of older folks mourning the decline of the church they love.

Vibrant, fruitful, growing congregations have been willing to say *Yes* to things that declining congregations have said *No* to. They lead in mission, outreach, and growth because they've dared to do things that their peers have been unwilling to do. They've discovered that change is necessary and that risk is healthy. A culture of *Yes*, of possibility and of calling and of boldness, overcomes a culture of *No*, and people feel empowered and encouraged to greater ministry for the purposes of Christ.

A Sense of Imperative

Some months ago, my wife and I visited a hardware store to look for patio furniture. We found the perfect set that included a table and four chairs, but we only wanted two chairs. The price tag listed a total for the entire set as well as a price for each individual piece, including each chair, and so we told a service representative that we would like to buy two chairs. He returned from the storage area a few minutes later to tell us we couldn't buy just two because the chairs were in a box with four together. We had to buy the whole set, or nothing.

Since the price tag gave the individual price for each chair, I thought this implied that someone could purchase any number of chairs. He was adamant that since the chairs were in a box of four that he could not sell them separately. I politely asked if he could ask a manager, but he gave several reasons why he couldn't do that. My wife and I looked around at other chairs, but none fit our purposes as well as those we had already found. After a few minutes, we went to another service representative to ask whether we could buy the chairs. He immediately returned with the two chairs, and we bought them.

The job of both store clerks was to sell these chairs, and we wanted to buy them. Both of them were trained and paid to satisfy customers and sell patio furniture. In fact, their job was to encourage us and help us to purchase merchandise, and both of them would have found satisfaction in meeting our needs and perhaps received a commission for doing so. But one of them allowed the slightest inconvenience or uncertainty to shut down the transaction. He was saying *No* to an easy and obvious sale when sales were his purpose.

The same thing happens in churches—small groups are denied use of the facility because the church would have to loan the key; confusing signs frustrate newcomers and leave them wandering around lost; mission teams are prohibited from using the kitchen because they might lose the flatware; children are prohibited from playgrounds because they're not our own kids. We lose sight of our mission.

Congregations lose their sense of imperative. They forget their purpose, or they allow a thousand lesser concerns to obscure their mission. Congregations without a clear sense of imperative get so caught up in their own habits and preferences that they find themselves saying *No* when the slightest obstacle or inconvenience arises. The most difficult kind of church to lead is a satisfied congregation that has little or no missional energy. You can't steer a parked car.

Imperative refers to the drive, passion, momentum, excitement, and desire that motivates ministry. A sense of imperative makes us want to experiment, try new things, do whatever it takes to overcome obstacles, and take the next step in our mission. Our imperative derives from our calling to serve God and our neighbors.

Congregations that cultivate a culture of *Yes* operate with a deeper sense of imperative, a clarity of mission. People know and believe in what their church is doing. They operate with the awareness that serving Christ requires our utmost and highest, and this awareness permeates the environment, stimulating our best energies and imagination.

Congregations with a sense of imperative believe that the work of Christ is absolutely necessary, vital to life and rebirth, and that inviting people into the spiritual life is something that must be done. They operate under the mandates of Christ, the imperatives that lace the teachings of Jesus: "Go. . . . Teach. . . . Heal. . . . Welcome. . . . Give. . . . Serve. . . . Pray. . . . Do. . . . Love. . . . Follow."

Imperative indicates urgency and importance: injustice must be righted, suffering relieved, people reached, lives changed. A sense of imperative focuses us on why we do what we do, which is to bring the good news that God has met our highest hopes and deepest needs in Jesus Christ. People who desperately need to hear this message and experience this truth live all around us.

A lost sense of imperative is fatal. Complacency and apathy robs the church of energy and passion and spirit. There's no drive, no momentum. People merely go through the motions, fulfilling their roles without a sense that their work really matters. Without a sense of imperative, strategies and mission statements fail to motivate, and the church remains immovable.

Regaining a sense of imperative is like finding an inhaler if you have asthma—you can breathe again, all fear is gone, and there's new energy and vitality.

Churches offer ministries that people need, and without them, many people remain disconnected from God, without the resources of faith and community, and empty of purpose and connection.

What do people need that congregations offer? Adam Hamilton, in *Leading Beyond the Walls*, reminds us that every church should be clear about the answers to the questions, "Why do people need Christ? Why do people need the church? And why do people need this particular congregation?"[2] Is it too presumptuous, self-righteous, or arrogant to perceive a responsibility, or even a calling, to invite and encourage others so that they may receive what we have received?

What do those of us who belong to a community of faith receive that our neighbors may need? Theologically, the answer may be, a relationship to God through Jesus Christ. This is too abstract for most; and for many, it feels heavy-laden with negative experiences of intrusive and aggressive evangelistic styles. The question persists, how do we express with integrity and clarity what we hope others receive? What do people need from the church?

People need to know God loves them, that they are of supreme value, and that their life has significance. People need to know that they are not alone, that when they face life's difficulties they are surrounded by a community of grace, that they do not have to figure out entirely for themselves how to cope with family tensions, self-doubts, periods of despair, economic reversal, and the temptations that hurt themselves or others. People need to know the peace that runs deeper than an absence of conflict, the hope that sustains them even through the most painful periods of grief, the sense of belonging that blesses them and stretches them and lifts them out of their own preoccupations. People need to learn how to offer and accept forgiveness and how to serve and be served. As a school for love, the church becomes a congregation where people learn from one another how to love. People need to know that life is more than having something to live on, but it is having something to live for, that life comes not from taking for oneself, but by giving of oneself. People need a sustaining sense of purpose.

Having said that, the last thing people want is to be told by someone else what they need! To invite people into Christ does not involve pounding people with "oughts" and "shoulds." Some people recognize their needs and search for meaning, for relationship, and for God. But most people discover their need for God's grace and for the love of Christ through the experience of receiving it. The stories are countless of people who did not know how hungry they were for genuine community until they experienced it, of people who never knew they needed the connection to God that worship fosters until they regularly attended, of people who sensed something was missing from their lives and didn't know what it was until they immersed themselves in regular service to others in need. When we invite people into a Bible study, or launch a Christian support group for single moms, or start a prayer ministry, or form a praise band, or begin a housing renovation project for the poor, or offer a food bank for families with young children, we are providing an avenue by which the spirit of God shapes the human soul. By such ministries, the spirit fills the empty spaces in people's lives, and God's inviting grace calls them out of themselves and into the world of Christ's service. The power of a congregation's ministry to change a person's life must never be underestimated! Perhaps that is how God changed each one of us.

Congregations reach people and draw them into life with Christ through the ministries they offer—worship services, children's programs, youth fellowships, service projects, Bible studies, support groups, mission initiatives, and justice ministries. Each of these begins with the calling of one person or a few people, and many eventually blossom into a calling that draws more people into service. These ministries change the lives of those they serve, and they change the lives of those who lead them. If a congregation's default answer to every initiative is *No* because of the attitudes of the leaders, the complexity of the systems, or the obstacles described above, then the church dampens its sense of imperative. It constricts ministry and restrains the callings of members rather than cultivating them.

We pray for more people to experience and share our ministry in Christ's name. This desire is unselfish; it is a purpose worth pouring our lives into, and it is the central purpose of the church. To desire more people in our churches does not make us small-minded, aggressive, strident, or intrusive. This is a desire for which our churches should be fervent, passionate, open, and unceasingly invitational.

A sense of imperative pulses through the stories of Jesus. At the outset of his ministry, Jesus says, "The Spirit of the Lord is upon me, because the Lord has anointed me. He has sent me to preach good news to the poor, to proclaim release to the prisoners and recovery of sight to the blind, to liberate the oppressed, and to proclaim the year of the Lord's favor" (Luke 4:18-19). Jesus says, "I came so that they could have life—indeed, life to the fullest" (John 10:10). He sent his disciples "on ahead in pairs to every city and place he was about to go" (Luke 10:1). After his death and resurrection, Jesus commissioned his disciples, commanding them to "Therefore, go and make disciples of all nations, baptizing them in the name of the Father and of the Son and of the Holy Spirit, teaching them to obey everything that I've commanded you" (Matt 28:18-20). Every conversation and encounter was imbued with purpose, the revealing of God's grace. The purpose of the church remains the same today, to teach and exemplify the love of God revealed in Christ. The Gospels vibrate with imperative, movement, purpose, initiative. The stories of Jesus leave little room for misunderstanding his urgency for us to work on his behalf.

Do You Want to Be Made Well?

The Gospel of John records the story of Jesus's encounter with a man lying beside the pool of Bethesda for thirty-eight years, hoping for healing and waiting for someone to move him into the pool when the waters stirred (John 5:1-8). Jesus saw him lying there and knew that he had been in the same place for a long time, and he said to him, "Do you want to get well?" We can perceive how incensed the man is by the question, and we can imagine him thinking, "Are you kidding? Are you making fun of me? I've been lying here wanting nothing more in the world than to be made well!" Isn't it obvious that he wants his situation changed so that he can break free from all that has restrained him for thirty-eight years? Jesus's question sounds almost cruel.

Jesus said, "Get up! Pick up your mat and walk" (John 5:8). At once the man was made well, and he took up his mat and began to walk.

This story has become symbolic of the many ways our churches and our people become constrained. Jesus confronts us with the question, "Do you want to get well?" In the face of change and transition, the answer is not simple. The question penetrates through layers of assumptions, complacencies, and fears that cause people to cling to a life that is incomplete or broken rather than to step into the uncertainty of change. People frequently oppose changing habits, attitudes, and values that hold themselves back and that restrain them from fulfilling the ministry of Christ for them or their church. As Ronald Heifetz has written, "Habits, values, and attitudes, even dysfunctional ones, are part of one's identity."[3]

To persuade people to give up the habits, attitudes, and systems that they know and feel comfortable with for habits, attitudes, and systems they've never experienced means convincing them to make a leap of faith in themselves and in life, the same leap of faith Jesus asked the paralyzed man to take. In effect, Jesus said, "Get up! Take your life situation and move with it."

Many churches operate with attitudes and systems that are no longer conducive to our mission, that shut down new ideas and restrain the capacities for ministry. They operate with a culture of *No*. Congregations have been lying paralyzed for decades, waiting and hoping for something to change.

"Do you want to get well?" Saying *Yes* means refashioning how we see ourselves and how we do our work. Creating a culture of *Yes* requires a leap of faith and a willingness to do things differently. It means letting ourselves be changed by the Spirit of God. The next few chapters suggest some ways for churches to answer *Yes* and move forward to a new future.

Questions for Reflection and Discussion

1. How did you become a part of the congregation to which you now belong? What services, ministries, small groups, or people opened the doors for you? What obstacles made it difficult for you to feel like you belonged?

2. How do you make sure that your church is not unintentionally hanging signs that say *"Do Not Enter"*?

3. When have you noticed a church using *Insider Language and Secret Codes* that caused you to have no idea what was being talked about?

4. How does your church assimilate people into small group ministries so that *The Middle Doors* remain open for new people? How could your church do better?

5. How "friendly" are your facilities for newcomers? For children? For the elderly? For people with physical disabilities? What suggestions for change would you offer?

6. When was a time that the way someone looked at you pushed you away and communicated that you were not welcome somewhere? When was a time that someone's smile made you feel like you belonged?

7. Are you aware of any *Shadow Missions*, unspoken values that drive ministry decisions, that limit conversations about change in your church?

8. Does the section ring true that describes the cumulative effect of *No*? How can your church avoid this path?

9. What sense of imperative drives the ministries of your congregation?

To Delve Deeper

Read Mark 10:13-16 or Matthew 19:13-15. Jesus becomes indignant at how his disciples are treating people and shooing away children who approach him, and he admonishes them not to put up obstacles that make it difficult for people to meet him. How does the church put up obstacles, intentionally or unintentionally, that make it difficult for people to approach Christ? What makes it difficult for newcomers from various backgrounds to enter into the life of your congregation? What could be done differently to make people feel that they belong?

Prayer

Lord, help us grab the initiative to treat others as we would want to be treated. Open our hearts, open our minds, open our doors. May we not miss the person you have prepared us to reach on your behalf, and not fail in the calling you have given us in Christ. Help us welcome one another as you have welcomed us, to the glory of God.

Chapter Four

Churches That Say Yes!

Changing Fundamental Assumptions

When Phil, a long-time member of the congregation, was diagnosed with Alzheimer's, his wife, Martha, searched for all the resources she could find to understand the disease. But books and online articles didn't go far enough. She felt increasingly overwhelmed as Phil's condition deteriorated. He required more and more personal care as his confusion, disorientation, and unpredictable behavior increased. The emotional toll was tremendous for Martha, as she became isolated, depressed, anxious, and exhausted. She felt supported by church members and pastors who reached out to her, but they couldn't understand what she was experiencing. Phil eventually required full-time, specialized care in a hospital-like facility, where he eventually passed away peacefully.

Several months following Phil's death, Martha approached the pastor and staff with an idea. She felt deeply called to help other spouses and adult children who have loved ones living with Alzheimer's.

Martha imagined the church offering a support group for family members of people with Alzheimer's. She had the organizational skills through her professional life and church service to coordinate such a group. The pastor and staff brainstormed with Martha about what resources might help, such as the presence of a psychologist or social worker. They talked about meeting times and places, launch dates, announcements and invitations to church members and to the general public. They shared the idea with other leaders for feedback. They discussed format, prayer support, hospitality, and follow-up.

Martha solicited the help of another church member, a professional family therapist, who volunteered her time to lead the group and to teach about the family dynamics and the emotional challenges of Alzheimer's families. Martha served as coordinator and convener, and provided the communications and hospitality. More than thirty people attended the first meeting, and only five of those had any previous relationship with the church. Participation grew large enough to form a second group that also met monthly. Because of the large Hispanic population in the area, Martha suggested a group for people who relied upon Spanish as their primary language. A counselor and a host were recruited to lead that group.

Over the years hundreds of people benefited from the Alzheimer's support groups, a ministry that began with a sense of calling, a desire to help, and the unique and personal experience that Martha offered to God.

When Donna and Bret discovered that she would give birth to triplets, the whole congregation celebrated with them. Everyone was also sobered by imagining what it must be like to bring home three infants when most couples feel overwhelmed with a single baby. The church secretary was one of many in the congregation who believed that the church must do something to support this burgeoning family. Volunteers stepped forward to form baby-sitting teams and the church held a diaper drive.

Others felt called to do more, and so volunteers for the children's ministry invited two couples who had twins to meet with a parent from the Day School who had triplets to ask them what might be helpful. These parents found such an immediate connection to each other that they later laughed at how all of them talked at once. They described how desperate, isolated, and overwhelmed they felt in the early months of being parents of twins, and how guilty they sometimes felt for feeling unfairly overwhelmed by circumstances that provided an incredible blessing. They wished they had had someone to talk to who understood what they were going through.

From that conversation a ministry was born, Twins and More, a support group for parents of twins, triplets, multiple births, and adoptions. Leaders felt called to offer a ministry of support to others who had experienced a challenge they themselves understood through personal experience. They contracted with a child development specialist to facilitate the first discussions. The ministry was announced through newsletters and websites for the church and day school, and the congregation placed invitations in local newspapers. Early gatherings had fifteen parents, which entailed nursery arrangements for nearly twenty children! Donna and Bret were among the beneficiaries of this vital ministry, which operated for a few years and then eventually closed as leaders moved on to other projects.

The Alzheimer's Support Group and Twins and More were not directly the fruit of a church strategy or a leadership planning retreat. Neither of these resulted from the work of a standing committee of elected leaders. Neither began with the pastor or the staff. They began with a sense of calling to serve God and with a personal passion to address a critical unmet need.

These ministries were consistent with the mission of the church and the priorities of the congregation. Both generated enough interest and resources to merit giving the ministry a chance. Both had leaders who worked collaboratively with other teams and with the church staff while also being entrusted with the authority to make essential decisions themselves and to resolve issues on-the-spot without asking anyone for permission. Both had personal champions for the cause and leaders gifted enough to organize and follow-through. Both reached people outside the membership of the congregation to address deep needs.

Neither idea passed through a large number of steps for approval. In fact, neither of them fits neatly into existing structures and responsibilities for most churches. Does an Alzheimer's support group or a ministry for parents of twins mostly comprised of nonmembers fit under the mission committee, the hospitality team, the congregational care committee, Christian education, or evangelism?

How did these ministries come to fruition if they were not the result of strategic planning or committee work? How can such ideas emerge and blossom in a congregation? What culture of support and encouragement calls forth such ministries?

Missional Assumptions

In the first chapter, we identified some faulty assumptions that restrain ministry, such as the beliefs that "this is our church," or "it's all about us," or "ideas come from the center." Imagine if we could infuse a congregation with a different set of assumptions through teaching, preaching, small groups, and leadership practices. Imagine if we could repeat and deepen and reinforce the following ideas:

Everyone Has Gifts for Ministry

From the earliest scriptures, Christian leaders have discerned that everyone who belongs to Christ and seeks to follow Christ is gifted by the Holy Spirit to contribute to the ministry of Christ. Just as everyone is part of the body of Christ with distinct functions to perform as the parts of a body—eye, mouth, ears—each serving a different purpose, so also everyone has spiritual gifts that the mission of Christ needs for strengthening the church and its witness.

Spiritual gifts are graces that individual Christians need to fulfill the mission of Christ through the church. They are described in various places in the New Testament, most notably in I Corinthians 12 and 13, Romans 12, and Ephesians 4. These scriptures highlight the gifts of administration, apostleship, compassion, discernment, encouragement, evangelism, exhortation, faith, giving, healing, helping, tongues, interpretation of tongues, knowledge, leadership, miracles, prophecy, servanthood, shepherding, teaching, and wisdom.

Each person brings to the mission of Christ a mix of spiritual gifts. Some gifts seem self-evidently relevant to leading and supporting the church, and others require digging through what appears to be archaic language in order to see their usefulness today.

Some spiritual gifts are so general as to belong to everyone. For instance, a measure of giving and helping and compassion should be cultivated in every follower of Christ through prayer and practice. But even in these areas, some people are particularly gifted to model and teach and mentor because giving and helping and compassion are natural to them.

Other spiritual gifts are less expected of all followers and more likely to be exercised in particular roles needed by the church, such as administration, leadership, teaching, or shepherding.

Widely available resources about spiritual gifts include study materials, assessment tools, workbooks, sermon ideas, and teaching plans for those who want to help people identify their spiritual gifts.

A focus on spiritual gifts reinforces the idea that ministry and the work of Christ do not belong exclusively to clergy. All who belong to Christ are encouraged to discover their gifts and to cultivate them for building up the church. Christ expects us to use our gifts.

Congregations that operate with the assumption that everyone is gifted for some form of ministry regularly teach and preach on spiritual gifts and offer small group activities that include assessments and inventories to help people identify their gifts and discern how best to use them. People often discover that they do not see gifts in themselves that others see in them. Through prayerful conversation and contemplation, a supportive community helps people identify, cultivate, and use their gifts in meaningful and helpful ways.

Assessment tools for spiritual gifts are not personality inventories, tests, or examinations that receive a grade. Rather, they involve personal exploration in a context of encouragement. They are a means of intentionally inviting the Holy Spirit deeply into the life of the church and into the ministry of the persons who participate. A good conversation about spiritual gifts sparks "aha" moments and new insights as people reflect on God's activity in their lives.

Repeating and reinforcing the idea that all members of the body of Christ are gifted by the Holy Spirit for the strengthening of the church results in new energy, insight, encouragement, and discovery. People reflect more deeply on their relationship with God, and they develop a vocabulary for identifying the positive contribution to ministry that God desires them to make. It stimulates dialogue about the many diverse ways God uses people to serve and lead. A focus on spiritual gifts releases people for ministry.

People with the same spiritual gifts may use them for the ministry of the church in radically different ways. An eighty-five-year-old living in a nursing care center, a middle-aged store clerk, and a young lawyer who all share the gifts of hospitality and helping will necessarily use them differently than will a fourteen-year-old student with the same gifts. But all of them can use their spiritual gifts in a way that builds up the body of Christ and extends the witness of the church.

God Calls Everyone to Service and Ministry

A second missional assumption is that everyone who belongs to the body of Christ is called by God to ministry. With our baptism, we are drawn into the work of Christ, and as we grow in grace and seek to follow Christ, God beckons us into serving.

Often Christians use the language of "called to ministry" too narrowly, applying it only to those people who pursue full-time Christian service in some form of ordained, licensed, or certified ministry. But every Christian is entrusted with the work of ministry through their baptism and profession of faith.

God's call shapes us in small ways every day. Seeking to follow Christ affects how we relate to our families, what kind of friend and coworker we are, the sort of neighbor and citizen we become. God calls us to build up rather than to tear down, to foster justice rather than to treat people unfairly, to help those in need rather than disregard them.

God also calls us to bold and audacious ministries. God's call causes us to go places we might not choose to go if left to our own preferences. It's not that we literally hear a Hollywood-like voice from God booming out loud in clearly resonant tones. Rather, our relationship with Christ, our prayer life, our participation in worship, or our study of scripture stimulates an inner urge or strong impulse. God awakens us to a particular sense of responsibility to act. We become aware of an unmet need even as we become aware of the particular gifts, passions, and experiences we ourselves can offer to address the need on behalf of Christ.

In *Wishful Thinking*, Frederick Buechner describes God's call to service and ministry as "the place where your deep gladness and the world's deep hunger meet."[1]

Picture a graph-like matrix. Along the left side of the graph are all the deep human needs, sufferings, and challenges that require bold and courageous service. These are the areas God needs people to work.

Along the bottom of the graph are all the particular gifts and passions and interests that characterize your life. These are the things that personally motivate you. Somewhere on the graph, unmet needs that God wants addressed intersect with your own personal interests, gifts, and passions, and that's where you find yourself offering effective help. That's where you take your place in God's service, making a difference in ways you find satisfying.

If someone responds only to needs for which they have no passion, they work slave-like for purposes that do not compel them. On the other hand, if they disregard the world's needs, and only do what they want to do, then they risk offering ministry that is irrelevant and ineffective for God's purposes, or they serve themselves rather than responding to God's call.

Hundreds of scriptural stories and teachings invite us to open ourselves to God's call to serve others: "Then Jesus went to work on his disciples. 'Anyone who intends to come with me has to let me lead. You're not in the driver's seat; *I* am. Don't run from suffering; embrace it. Follow me and I'll show you how. Self-help is no help at all. Self-sacrifice is the way, my way, to finding yourself, your true self'" (Matt 16:24-25 *The Message*).

Jesus said, "Whoever wants to become great must become a servant.... That is what the Son of Man has done: He came to serve, not be served—and then to give away his life" (Matt 20:27-28 *The Message*).

Scripture goes so far as to suggest that to encounter Jesus Christ face-to-face in the most tangible way, the whole reality he embodies, involves serving another person by relieving suffering through feeding the hungry, clothing the naked, visiting the imprisoned, and welcoming the stranger. "I'm telling the solemn truth: Whenever you did one of these things to someone overlooked or ignored, that was me—you did it to me" (Matt 25:40 *The Message*).

Responding to God's call does not merely involve helpful activities that make a difference; Christ-like service helps us become the persons God created us to be. It fulfills God's hope and will for us.

By responding to God's call to serve others, we bear witness that the life and teaching of Jesus are true, that fullness of life is discovered in the giving and not in the taking, that abundance is found in loving rather than in fearing, that happiness comes in opening ourselves to others rather than by closing ourselves off.

The real you, your true self, is discovered in letting Christ lead you into serving others with compassion. In serving, we mediate the grace of God. The unsolicited, unconditional love of God that we receive flows through us to others. God's purpose permeates our lives. As God's love runs through us, we see Jesus Christ more clearly; we work with him and he works through us. Serving puts Jesus's love into practice, and the ultimate reality we see in Christ becomes tangible once again, revealed as a force and power in the world. Serving others, we live the truth.

Imagine how adopting these two assumptions—that everyone has been gifted by the Holy Spirit for strengthening the church, and that God calls everyone to ministry—can change a church. A new energy is released. Leadership is not about controlling or restraining or holding meetings; it's about helping people discover their gifts and fulfill their ministries. These assumptions unleash people for ministry.

The Ministries of the Church Should Foster Spiritual Growth and Discipleship

Disciple is derived from *discipulus* and *discere*, words that mean *learner* and *follower*. A disciple of Jesus Christ is someone who desires to follow Christ, who believes in his teachings and tries to act and live accordingly.

If the primary purpose of the church is to form disciples—helping people grow in grace and in knowledge and love of God through Christ—then every ministry should be tied to that purpose. Each ministry offered by the church should help people become disciples of Jesus Christ—to witness to Jesus Christ in the world and to follow his teachings through acts of compassion, justice, worship, and devotion under the guidance of the Holy Spirit.[2]

Many churches offer an array of activities for people to participate in without delving deeply into questions of intentionality. What do we believe a mature disciple looks like, and are our ministries fostering growth toward that? Do we have a goal in mind?

Those who belong to the body of Christ are at differing stages in following Christ and in spiritual development. One pastor describes his perception that about 40 percent of those who belong to the church are rather casual about their Christian identity. Their spiritual commitments have relatively little impact on shaping their lives, their attitudes, thoughts, emotions, or action. They consider themselves Christian, go to church now and then, pray when they are in trouble, and help out occasionally.

Another 30 percent are more engaged, more regular in worship, generally supportive of the church, and occasionally participate in Bible studies or service projects. They take their faith more seriously and their relationship with God shapes their lives in visible ways. Another 20 percent are further along in their discipleship, and they tithe or give generously enough that it affects their spending and saving patterns; they regularly attend worship even when they have to adapt their schedules to do so; they belong to small groups such as Bible studies or classes, and they frequently give generous amounts of time to serving and leading. Their spiritual life forms an essential part of their identity.

The pastor rather boldly asserts that there is a final 10 percent that are further along the path toward sanctification. These disciples are not crippled by obvious sinful patterns, are devoted in personal prayer life and community worship, are attentive to the needs and injustices of the world and offer themselves generously to help, are attentive to God and demonstrate significant growth in the fruit of the spirit—gentleness, kindness, patience.

Anyone who thinks himself or herself in the final category definitely is not! The law of spiritual relativity says that the closer you grow to Christ, the further you feel from Christ's perfect love.[3]

The benefit of thinking about the spiritual journey is that it helps us focus on what we hope happens to someone who belongs to a congregation over the course of time. Such a conversation inserts the notion of intentionality to our ministries. Do our ministries help people at these various stages of faith to move closer to Christ, to grow in Christ, to become more Christ-like in their daily lives and in serving their neighbor? Do we have an end in mind?

We see similar stages of discipleship in scriptures. A number of passages describe large crowds that gather around to hear Jesus. Scripture reports five thousand people present for the Sermon on the Mount and four thousand for the miracle of the seven loaves. Luke describes how "a crowd of thousands upon thousands gathered" (Luke 12:1). But nowhere does scripture suggest that all those thousands changed their lives significantly to follow Christ. Instead, scripture reports how Jesus sent out the seventy to every town and place where he himself intended to go, a group that no doubt reshaped their lives significantly to fulfill that calling. The Gospels describe a smaller handful of women and men who completely gave themselves over to following Christ.

A fundamental missional assumption that undergirds healthy ministries is that our programs help people grow in discipleship and that we are going to put our resources into ministries that genuinely change lives. Ministries should help people grow in Christ and not merely keep them busy. Our programs will not merely be activities we do because another church is doing them or because we've always done things this way. Instead, we will offer ministries that help people grow in grace become more compassionate, generous, given to service, attentive to God, knowledgeable about their faith, and willing to share it.

Churches that operate with this missional assumption invest time in developing a discipleship plan. They review their ministries regularly to evaluate how each contributes to growth in Christ. They consciously balance high-quality ministries that help people know scripture and theology with those that give people experience with serving and with those that deepen the personal devotional life through worship and prayer. They provide ministries that place people in the most advantageous circumstances to be shaped by grace. They help people cooperate with the Holy Spirit in their own growth in grace. They develop ministries that draw people toward Christ and toward loving God by serving their neighbors. They offer the hospitality of Christ, not to encourage people to change their memberships but so that the love of Christ changes people's lives. Everything is tied to the purpose of forming disciples and equipping them for ministry.

The Church's Mission Is Outward-Focused

Churches exist, not for the insiders but for the outsiders. The moment the church begins to operate entirely for the benefit of those who already belong, it loses its missional focus and begins to die. The Holy Spirit works through the ministries of the church to form disciples of Jesus Christ *for the transformation of the world,* not merely for the benefit and satisfaction of the followers themselves.

Jesus formed a group of disciples that followed him from place to place, learning and receiving the grace he offered. But even with a cadre of believers following him, listening to him, and sharing meals with him, whom did Jesus focus on? He continually drew the attention of his followers to those outside the community—the tax-collectors, the lepers, the Roman soldiers, the foreigners, the sick, the poor, and the people who were blind.

A critical role of leadership in the church is to maintain outward focus and to direct the energies of the church toward the mission field. The mission of the church is not fulfilled at church meetings and administration councils; at best, these are places to focus on the mission and plan how to fulfill it. The mission of the church is fulfilled as those who belong to Christ serve, invite, and engage those who do not belong to the church. The mission field includes the people in the surrounding neighborhood and community as well as those in special need throughout the world.

When considering a new ministry idea, the driving questions are not merely about how it affects those already present. Instead, questions include: How will this ministry idea make a difference in the lives of people? How will it extend the witness of Christ in the world? How will this ministry reach other people who do not belong to the church? How might this ministry become a doorway for those outside the community of faith to enter into a relationship with the church?

Vibrant, fruitful, growing churches invest as much attention, energy, focus, and prayer on those outside the congregation as they do upon those who belong to the community of faith. They take hospitality seriously, looking at every aspect of their ministry, facility, and worship services from the point of view of visitors and guests. They practice radical hospitality and refuse to settle for mediocrity. They overcome obstacles that make participation by visitors difficult. They regularly evaluate issues of accessibility for people with disabilities, monitor the content and tone of signage, treat visitors as if they are welcoming friends into their own homes, and regularly review their communications to see that their messages are inviting and understandable. They welcome visitors with utmost joy and delight, and do everything they can to help them assimilate into the life of the congregation. They consciously shift from "what's in it for me?" to "how can I help you?" at every opportunity.

The Work of the Church Is to Encourage People in Their Callings

Making disciples is not the same as recruiting new members. Forming disciples involves developing people in their ministries, encouraging them in their spiritual journeys, helping them to discover their gifts and to discern their callings. Part of our task as disciples is to be attentive to the gifts and callings in others, to name them and to foster them.

The purpose of committees is not merely to hold meetings and to provide activities to fill the calendar. The work of leading a community of faith is not to narrow options for ministry or make sure everyone participates in what is currently offered, but to increase opportunities to learn, serve, and grow in Christ. The purpose of leadership is not to close doors but to open them; not to control everyone but to encourage everyone in ministry.

Leaders have to give people permission to take seriously their spiritual gifts and their sense of calling to a ministry. A person beginning to discern her gifts, especially if she is new to a community of faith, feels vulnerable, self-conscious, and unsure. A person sharing a sense of calling may offer his idea with great tentativeness. They feel like the person in the scary movie walking through the dark house alone with a single candle. They try to protect it with their hand as they walk forward into the unknown. The candle can blow out easily, and the flame is always just a breath away from being extinguished. Dense and complex committee structures or critical and negative leaders make the task of nurturing a calling seem impossible. The ministry of encouragement by church leaders means helping the person protect the flame and continually rekindle the passion as they move forward in their Christian walk.

The church is a school for love, helping people grow in grace and in the knowledge and love of God. It's a community of mission, equipping and sending people into their daily lives for service and witness. It is a family of support, of welcome and hospitality for strangers, of caring for people and sharing Christ's love through all the joys and grieving of life. The work of the church is helping people take the next step in their orientation toward Christ, no matter where they might be on their journey. The purpose of the church is more about placing people in the optimum circumstance to be formed by the grace of Christ through service, fellowship, prayer, and worship than about placing them on the right committees.

These missional assumptions derive from scriptural witness. Jesus spoke about how God works in the world, and people listened. He invited people to follow him, and many did. He sent them out to pray and teach and love, and gave them countless models and stories about what it means to look at the world through God's eyes and do the kingdom work God desires. He welcomed strangers and reached out to others who refused to engage. He highlighted practices of discipleship, such as the widow and her coins, Martha in her service, and Mary in her devotion, and he challenged the rich on their treatment of the poor and for their reliance upon worldly wealth. He described the compassionate impulses of the Samaritan, the wisdom of building on a firm foundation, the folly of clinging to worldly goods.

Jesus never proposed steps or committees or organizational structures. Instead, he provided hundreds of teachings about the practice of ministry and the importance of feeding the hungry, giving water to the thirsty, visiting the incarcerated, and searching for the lost. The sign of a life changed by grace was the evident desire to follow him, serve others, and honor God. And Jesus repeatedly used the metaphor of fruitfulness to describe the impact and outcome of ministry: "My Father is glorified when you produce much fruit and in this way prove that you are my disciples" (John 15:8). Disciples of Jesus Christ were identified by their fruit for the kingdom, the difference made in the lives of people, and the shaping of communities. Everything had a purpose: to draw people toward God and to empower them for service in God's kingdom.

Churches that share these missional assumptions expect people to have ideas, dreams, hopes, and passions for ministry. Rather than being unprepared to respond to new ideas or surprised when people feel called to a ministry, they expect people to be called by God to work for Christ in their daily lives, their families and communities, and in their church. Churches that operate with these assumptions encourage people to share their callings, and they work with people to refine, shape, and bring their callings to fruition.

In many churches, cultivating the call to ministry begins when someone first enters the life of the church. During classes for new members, leaders introduce the idea of spiritual gifts and suggest that everyone has a ministry even as they describe the array of learning and service opportunities offered by the congregation. Some churches invite people to complete a spiritual gifts inventory and offer to meet personally with each person to help match gifts to opportunities to serve. They welcome the ideas and callings of newcomers.

When churches operate under these assumptions, leaders foster imagination and motivate ministry rather than trying to fit every person into existing ministries. They shape support structures to fit ministry rather than force new ministry ideas to fit the framework of existing structures.

In growing churches, ministry ideas seldom begin with committees. Instead, they emerge from the real life experiences of people, including many people who will never serve on a church committee. Ideas emerge as people grow in discipleship. Fruitful churches operate with assumptions that set people free to fulfill their callings.

Fruitful churches provide open avenues for people to express their callings and to experiment with new ideas. They work to multiply ministry rather than to control it. They clarify the mission, identify priorities, set the boundaries of appropriate behavior and accountability, and then allow people to self-organize. Fruitful churches set free groups of people who discern a common calling and passion.

Fundamental Questions

These missional assumptions change the fundamental questions that drive the congregation and that form the culture of leadership.

Instead of asking prospective members, "What role in the life of the church would you like to take on?" or, "What committee do you want to serve on?"

churches that operate with missional assumptions shift to questions such as "Tell me about a ministry you have felt God calling you to fulfill. What difference do you feel God is calling you to make? What gifts and skills and passions do you have for ministry?"

The responses to these questions are as varied as the people who are asked, and may lead to ministries that the church has never considered. One person may describe their calling to provide transportation for the elderly and another will talk about how their life has prepared them to deal with difficult, resistant, conflicted, and rebellious youth. Another will describe their desire to stay in the background, supporting the church through helping ministries that deal with the daily necessities that help a church thrive, such as folding bulletins, setting up chairs, maintaining the shrubbery. Others will describe their gift of music and singing, and others may share their multicultural experience or their bilingual abilities in order to offer themselves to serve with mission teams.

Instead of the question, "What committee do we take this to?" missional churches ask, "Who are the other people who share this interest, passion, and calling, and how do we connect with them?"

Instead of, "How much does this cost?" or, "Where do we find money in the budget?" the question becomes "What are we willing to give to see this ministry through? What costs are those who feel called willing to pay?"

Instead of focusing on "What are the reasons this can't be done in our church?" the conversation shifts to "What are the assets and resources and who are the people that align for this task?"

Instead of an attitude among leaders that asks, "How do we get them to do what we want?" or, "How do we make them change?" a shift toward, "What changes are we willing to make in ourselves and what are we willing to do?"

Instead of strategy sessions and long-term planning teams that focus principally on steps, structures, and flow-charts, a shift occurs toward changing the culture to become permission-giving rather than prerogative-protecting. Instead of "you ought," the language shifts to "we will."

Instead of a church driven by committees, the church shifts toward ministry driven by callings. Instead of a calendar full of meetings, the calendar fills with opportunities for serving, learning, and worship.

Instead of asking, "What's in it for us?" the church shifts its focus to the unmet needs of the community around it, asking, "What can we offer?" Instead of demanding that their own preferences and tastes take precedent, they attend to the needs of newcomers.

Instead of good ideas beginning at the center and being pushed throughout the church, the leadership shifts toward a model of receiving ideas from the margins, refining them, and then inviting people from throughout the church to participate as they feel called to do.

Instead of leadership meetings filled with reporting and rehashing, the agendas shift toward learning and leading. Rather than leaders concerned about controlling, leadership shifts toward getting things done.

Instead of asking people to fill vacancies on committees, the church shifts to inviting people to lead through personal, prayerful conversation. Pastors and lay leaders ask prospective leaders to pray about whether they sense God is calling them to serve in this way, and they describe why they discern that God may have prepared them for this task because of their spiritual gifts, natural aptitudes, or life experience. The nominations process shifts from being a mechanical task of filling vacancies to a process of discernment for the good of the mission of the church.

Drawn into Greater Ministry

Imagine a church that invests incredible energy in helping people discover their callings and to use their spiritual gifts for building up the church. Everyone is called to serve. Some respond by participating in ministries initiated by church staff and leaders. Others form ministries together with those who share common passions or interests. Others notice unmet needs in the community or world, and they initiate ministries, inviting others to help. Some encourage and mentor and cultivate the callings of other people.

"What in the world am I doing here? I can't tell you how many times I've found myself asking that question during the last several years." That's how Ken begins his story about the unusual and unexpected places his faith journey has taken him since he discovered his calling.[4]

Ken is a medical technician in his mid-fifties, a husband and father, and a handyman. He belongs to a congregation where he has attended worship and an adult Bible class for twenty-five years. "The first thing I helped with was the Thanksgiving baskets," he says. The church gathered canned goods, purchased perishables, and delivered boxes to families in need. The ministry was simple, helpful, and required little time. It afforded Ken his first glimpse at life on the other side of town and caused him to step into the homes of people he never would have otherwise met. He mostly remembers the team spirit and getting to know other volunteers.

Later, when the youth group worked on a week-long housing rehab project, Ken took a day off from his job, brought his tools, and worked alongside the young people. "I remember the impact the project made on the youth, and I recall meeting the family whose house we were re-roofing. I felt like we were making a difference that mattered. I helped with the project each summer after that." A few years later, the congregation launched a hands-on ministry that involved a three-day weekend commitment from work teams to build wheelchair ramps, redo flooring, and reroof homes for families referred to them by a social service agency. Ken served as a team member the first year, and as a team leader in the years that followed. "That project changed how I viewed our work," he says, "and I realized it was about connecting with the people we were serving, and not just about laying tiles or pouring concrete. I met an elderly woman and her disabled son living in desperate conditions, and as we were working together, I found myself thinking about my own lifestyle and all the trappings that we call necessities. You can't really understand your own circumstances without knowing how most of the world lives."

Eventually, Ken received training and led a volunteer work team to Nicaragua where he slept on a church floor in a remote village that had no electricity or running water. The team rebuilt a school damaged by a hurricane, and they taught children. Ken's perceptions of how citizens from wealthy countries relate to those from third world countries became more nuanced. "That trip shattered myths for me about what makes for a good life. Not everyone wants to be like us, and we have much to learn about community, hospitality, simplicity, and stewardship of resources from other people. I found myself amazed by the beauty of living simply."

Can you see the growth that is taking place as Ken matures in discipleship and in his calling? From Thanksgiving baskets to wheelchair ramps to constructing houses to projects in Central America to teaching others, Ken's journey has taken him places he could never have imagined and connected him with an amazing diversity of people. "At first, it was about the roof, the sink, the work. Then it was about team members and the friendships formed with other volunteers. Later, it was about the people served and the privilege of working alongside them. And then it was about influencing policies to relieve suffering. At every step for me, it's been about growing in Christ." Now he mentors new members who want to get involved with hands-on service projects. "I never imagined myself doing this," he says. "But it helps answer the question, 'What in the world am I here for?' This is one of the reasons God put me here."

Ken followed a path that fit his spiritual gifts, his context, and his passions. He discovered his calling in Christ and responded. His service has changed the lives of countless people, and it has formed him. God has used Ken's service to change him from the inside out.

Other people's pathways differ dramatically, and yet follow a similar trajectory. When followers say *Yes* to God's calling, and the church says *Yes* to fostering ministry, people feel free to experiment. They help with a service project or lead a prayer team or start a Bible study. They catch the spirit, noticing the difference their work makes for others and for themselves. They mature and gain confidence, branch out or deepen their commitment, and with the passage of time and a pattern of service, they end up somewhere totally unexpected, making a difference in significant and lasting ways. As they grow in discipleship, their own inner maturing in Christ transforms the lives of other people and changes the world.

Shirley's volunteer stint for a women's shelter working with survivors of domestic violence opened the door for her service on their board of directors. The connections she made matched other passions she had, and she began to use her board-acquired skills to support a literacy program for children, which led to her certification to teach volunteers at a literacy center, which has led to her involvement in community and school district educational initiatives. As she's discovered her own ministry, she's drawn others from her church into service. And her witness has served as a doorway to those unrelated to the church to enter the community of faith for the first time.

Ana's volunteer teaching of elementary classes for Sunday school led to her helping with a weeklong Vacation Bible School program in cooperation with an inner city church that reaches out to families with single moms. She loved it, and formed relationships with the women that led to her volunteer work in a jobs training program and the establishment of an urban child-care program. She felt supported by her church and has helped others begin to serve alongside her.

Lynn's ministry of prayer and Tom's gift of encouragement changed the culture of their congregation. Lynn formed a prayer team that met weekly to pray for each member of the church and for every ministry the church offered. Later, Lynn took on the role of mentor for women new to the congregation, meeting one-on-one with each person to invite, encourage, answer questions, and offer support. Tom had no particular interest or aptitude for hands-on service projects or teaching, but he loved the church. He came to discern that his role was to support the ministries of others on the front lines. His generous financial gifts made ministry possible, and his positive, faithful, and encouraging voice in leadership gave people the support and permission to take on bold projects. When Tom said, "That's a great idea. We can do that," everyone listened and felt encouraged.

After Lance's retirement, he helped with a "cleanup day" around the church with other retirees. He enjoys working outdoors with his hands, and he saw the need for more consistent care and repair for the church facilities. He and a friend worked together twice a month, trimming trees, planting bushes, painting doors, fixing leaks. He was asked to serve on the Grounds Committee. Now he tends the cemetery, too, recruiting other retirees to help.

Ruth was in her late seventies when her husband died and she fell into a severe depression. She lived alone and knew hardly anyone in the community. A neighbor invited the pastor to meet with her. The pastor spoke with her about her depression, loneliness, and disconnection, and encouraged her to consult her doctor. He also invited her to volunteer in the church office. Overcoming internal resistance, she showed up to answer the phone and to greet visitors. She rediscovered long-neglected skills she had developed as an office worker decades before, and began to organize tasks in ways that helped the church. She became the support person for volunteers, coordinating communication for work teams that rebuild houses, feed the homeless, and visit shut-ins. She practices a remarkable gift of encouragement.

Earl was new to the faith when he attended a *Walk to Emmaus* retreat. He experienced a powerful personal transformation that led him to volunteer with future retreats. After two years of supporting and leading *Emmaus*, he felt called to help with *Kairos* prison-based retreats. He served on a planning team and then spent a weekend locked down with inmates to offer the retreat for them. The experience changed him, and he became active with victims' rights organizations and prison reform agencies.

Sondra occasionally used her nursing skills to support weekend work projects at her urban church that has an active ministry for the homeless, for addicts, and for people living with HIV. She served food at the shelter, distributed clothes, and assisted people in locating housing. She also raised money to support her congregation's partner church in Mozambique. When she had the opportunity to visit Mozambique, the experience changed her life. She became passionate about health-care issues in Africa, raising funds for malaria nets, and working as an advocate on world-health issues and the diseases of poverty. She has spoken to dozens of churches and helped other people catch the spirit of serving the poorest of the poor.

What in the world am I doing here? One thing leads to another leads to another. That's the way it works with the call of Christ to ministry. With a disciplined pattern of serving and of opening themselves afresh to following

Christ, all of these persons have ended up somewhere they could never have imagined. They felt supported and encouraged by their congregations rather than restrained or limited. They were drawn into ministry. They are each making a real difference in the lives of others, and they are changing the part of the world God has given them to change.

Using their spiritual gifts and discovering their callings changes the lives of those who offer ministry. It changes the lives of those who receive ministry. It changes the world as we share directly with God in the creating and re-creating work that makes all things new.

A Guided Autonomy

These examples of people unleashed for ministry demonstrate the diversity of callings and gifts that God uses for extending the witness of the church. They are all consistent with the mission of the church and with the priorities of the congregation. They all derived from prayerful discernment about unmet human needs and from a growing awareness of the passions and interests of people to serve. Each of these people became champions and supporters of the ministries they offered in a way that drew other people into helping. These ministries were outward-focused, transforming the world by changing people's lives by the grace of God. They are fruitful, exhibiting a real impact for the purposes of Christ. The role of the church in each instance was to give permission rather than to control. Pastors and leaders gave people permission to pursue their passions.

These examples represent congregations practicing *a guided autonomy* in its support of ministries rather than a restraining and controlling influence. The approach is *guided* because the ministries are evaluated against the mission of the church and the priorities of the congregation, and they are held to high expectations of excellence, fruitfulness, and accountability. They fit the purpose of helping people grow in discipleship.

The approach represents an *autonomy* because people discover their gifts and discern their callings in the context of supportive community rather than having to fit into existing programs. They are free to organize with others to initiate ministries that meet unaddressed needs that are consistent with the church's mission. Team leaders are closer to the situation and know the context best and are capable of making decisions with collaboration and with informal conversations rather than through formal systems. The church becomes more responsive to the contemporary needs of people than to traditions, customs, and structures. Ministries have a self-generating quality within a supportive community of conversation, collaboration, learning, and encouragement. People with the same interests and callings are free to operate with a minimum of restraint and without having their passions dampened by endless permission-seeking steps in a complex committee structure. The church removes as many obstacles to ministry as possible.

Churches that operate with the missional assumptions outlined in this chapter eventually reflect a guided autonomy. Leaders of ministries do not feel abandoned, but supported. Neither do they feel controlled, but rather they receive encouragement.

If leaders allow these missional assumptions to drive their decisions, then nearly any structural or organizational system can become more permission giving. A change of attitudes and values leads to a change in organizational behavior. All kinds of new ideas emerge as people are set free for ministry, and the work of the church multiplies and becomes more fruitful. However, some churches take permission-giving to another level by actually changing their systems and not just their assumptions and attitudes, and it's to these churches that we turn our attention next.

Questions for Reflection and Discussion

1. What ministries have had the greatest impact in shaping your own growth in discipleship? How has belonging to a congregation shaped your life? How are you a different person because of your participation in worship, community, and service at your church?

2. If your congregation more fully embraced the assumptions that everyone has spiritual gifts and that God calls everyone to serve, how would this change how your church thinks about ministry?

3. Which of the five missional assumptions described in this chapter drive the planning of ministry in your congregation?

4. What gifts do you bring to the ministry of Christ? How have you detected the calling of God to serve in your own life?

5. Can you think of additional examples of people who ask themselves, "What in the world am I doing here?" because of the unexpected way they've been drawn by God into greater ministry? Where's the most unexpected place serving God has ever taken you?

To Delve Deeper

Read Luke 4:16-21, Matthew 28:16-20, and the many "I am" statements by Jesus in the Gospel of John (I am the bread, the good shepherd, the light, the gate, the resurrection, the vine, the life, the way, the truth). What is the sense of imperative that is implied in each example?

Prayer

Consecrate our congregation, dear God, to your purposes. Lead us to the rediscovery of wonder, awe, peace, joy, and life that comes with being part of the body of Christ. May people see in us the presence of Christ, and may Christ reach out through us to a hurting world.

Chapter Five

Systems That Say Yes!

Becoming a Permission-Giving Church

In 1919, a young army officer was given the task of moving a large convoy of military equipment from the East Coast of the United States to the West Coast, a distance of 3,251 miles. The heavy trucks meandered from town to town and wound through tiny streets of small communities. Narrow bridges, impassable main streets, and unpaved roads obstructed and redirected their progress. The convoy took sixty-two days to complete its journey, reporting two-hundred and thirty road incidents, breakdowns, and extrications, losing nine heavy trucks, injuring nineteen personnel.

The army officer who led the convoy believed this represented a critical threat to national security. He thought the army should be able to move equipment and troops from one coast to another or from one border to another in forty-eight hours. He proposed a solution that was never adopted—until he himself became president of the United States nearly forty years later. President Dwight D. Eisenhower signed into law the Interstate Highway System.

How does a good idea in your congregation travel from initial inspiration to fruitful ministry? Does the path meander through narrow roadways and impassable bridges with a thousand stops, a hundred obstacles, and lots of casualties? Or do ideas flow through the system like cars speeding down the freeway?

Adopting missional assumptions has the effect of making any church organizational system more effective, outward focused, and purpose driven. Even if a church never changes a single committee but succeeds in changing the attitudes of leaders, the congregation becomes more fruitful and effective.

After careful deliberation, some churches go the second mile. They determine their organizational structure itself is asphyxiating, unduly mechanistic, restraining, slow, and inconsistent with their mission. They rethink church operations with the intention of becoming more agile, responsive, and permission giving.

73

Complexity is the silent killer of organizations. Bottlenecks and logjams can be avoided when we loosen up and unleash creative impulses. Simplicity works. Systems can say *Yes.*

The Dream Team

When Woods Chapel United Methodist Church in Lee's Summit, Missouri, moved into their new worship facility, average weekly attendance grew from 350 to 500 people. The pastor, Jeff Brinkman, and congregational leaders knew they had to change their organizational and operational systems or they would lose momentum. Systems that worked moderately well before the growth were now sluggish, convoluted, and confusing. Decisions required too many meetings, steps, and approvals. Woods Chapel contracted with a consultant who suggested streamlining processes, reducing the number and size of committees, and creating a permission-giving environment to replace the traditional multistep permission-seeking structure that was so slow and frustrating.[1]

After much planning and conversation, the church adopted thirty-five motions at one church-wide meeting to radically reorganize the governance and structure of the church. Leaders promised to operate under the new system for one year, and if it didn't work, the church would reinstitute previous operations.

Among the innovations was the creation of a Dream Team, a small group of elected laity and staff who met regularly to receive ideas for ministry from members. Anyone who cared about the church's ministry and wanted to attend was welcome. The work of the Dream Team was supplemented with a sustained focus on several themes through preaching and teaching: everyone is called to ministry, everyone grows in Christ through serving, and everyone has spiritual gifts useful to the church. Small groups and Bible studies focused on spiritual gifts inventories and on becoming more outward-focused. Sermons highlighted living outside oneself, becoming the hands and feet of Christ, and serving Christ by serving others.

The Dream Team met regularly to listen to people describe their calling to start new ministries. Ideas were sorted into three major areas for further conversation—inviting, growing, and sending. *Inviting* ministries related to hospitality, welcoming visitors, evangelism, assimilation, reaching out, helping people learn about or become more involved with the church. *Growing* related to learning experiences that deepened discipleship, such as support groups, Bible studies, adult Sunday school classes, youth and children's ministries, and other small group ministries that nurture faith and strengthen community. *Sending* has to do with mission, service, and justice ministries and the ways members make a positive difference by serving the neighborhood, city, and world. The Dream Team listens to and works with presenters to help them discern their callings and to answer three questions: How does this ministry fit the mission, values, and priorities of our church? Who is going to take responsibility for it? How will it be funded?

Over the next few years, more than thirty significant new ministries were launched. For example, one person felt called to provide home-cooked meals for parents staying at the Ronald McDonald House while their children were receiving cancer treatments. The presenter had six people willing to help and ready to go. Since volunteers prepared food at their own costs, the ministry had no funding implications for the church. The ministry was consistent with the mission of the church, aligned with the priorities and values of the congregation, and furthered the church's outreach into the community for parents facing stress, pain, and isolation. Once the ministry was adopted, other volunteers signed up to help.

Another person suggested that the church form a team of volunteers to work at a thrift shop one day a week that serves the homeless and low income families. She already had several friends who had expressed interest. About a dozen persons served weekly from a large pool of volunteers. The ministry continued for years until the coordinator moved away. Other volunteers offered to lead, but they were unable to give the time the founder had given, and the ministry grew less consistent. Eventually, the church had to tell the thrift shop that they could no longer provide volunteers for their assigned day each week. Woods Chapel ended their involvement. Woods Chapel was willing to allow the ministry to run its course and eventually to close when there were insufficient volunteers. When the conditions are right and there are enough people to volunteer and take responsibility for it, the ministry may start again.

Some ministries thrive, others die, and some undergo significant changes as they adapt and grow. Some involve hundreds of people and others engage only a few. Many are intentionally short-term, only lasting a few weeks or months to address a critical need. Like the parable of the sower, the outcomes are mixed, unpredictable, and uncertain. Nevertheless, a great harvest results.

The pastor confesses that he never liked the name Dream Team, but the practice of cultivating new ideas and of giving people permission to pursue their callings has been pivotal to his congregation's growth. Permission-giving means that leaders relinquish control. "I don't want to force ministry," Jeff says, "I simply want to get out of the way so ministry can happen."

Three Questions

The model used by Woods Chapel rests upon a foundation of prayer and discernment and relies upon three questions that must be answered sufficiently for a ministry to launch. The questions provide a template for discernment for leaders and staff.

A Foundation of Prayer, Discernment, and Calling. People who bring an idea are asked if they have prayed about it. How has this idea come to them? What mix of spiritual gifts does the work require? What gifts do they bring to the task? What are the indications that God has called them to this ministry and is calling the church to this ministry?

These questions assure that people don't simply suggest an idea because another church is doing it. The questions clarify motive and purpose. They protect the church from people who suggest something that they think the church should do but for which they themselves have no particular interest. Instead of "you ought to" or "the church ought to," the questions evoke, "I'm willing to" and "I'd like to."

Does It Align with the Mission?

The first question the Dream Team asks is, "Does the proposed ministry fit the mission, values, and priorities of the congregation?" Woods Chapel operates under the umbrella mission statement of the United Methodist Church—to make disciples of Jesus Christ for the transformation of the world. The congregation has refined the statement to highlight more directional words. Their mission statement reads *Woods Chapel: Connecting People to Jesus Christ*, and is broad enough for diverse interpretations but narrow enough to give direction for work. The mission derives from the premise that having a relationship to Christ and belonging to the body of Christ brings meaning, connection, and purpose, and helps members develop the qualities that matter in life—love, grace, peace, and hope. A sense of purpose permeates the congregation. A clearly stated mission and well-articulated values bring cohesion to the many autonomous expressions of ministry so that groups don't go in all directions at once. Ministries become mutually reinforcing rather than isolated and disconnected from the community.

If a group expresses an interest in forming a men's softball team, sponsoring a youth basketball league, launching a home Bible study, forming a mission team to restore homes after a tornado, or organizing a clothing drive for the homeless, they will have to describe how this activity connects people with Christ. What makes this a ministry and not merely a wholesome sports activity or community project? How does it express the love of Christ, draw people into the community of Christ, or represent Christ in the world? Does the ministry focus principally on the church's members or will it serve the neighborhood or target an at-risk group? What's the desired outcome, and how would it be evaluated?

These are critical components of alignment. The Dream Team does not merely offer an up or down vote on the proposed ministry. Instead, they help people refine the idea so that it more closely aligns with the mission. They help people understand the mission of the Woods Chapel. Those who initially suggest a sports team may have begun with the idea of enjoying community and building friendships. In conversation about the purpose of the church, they become aware of how the sports team could become a doorway into the life of the church.

Some suggestions are for good and positive activities, but they don't belong to the mission of the church. Other ideas clearly don't fit the priorities, purpose, or spirit of the congregation.

For instance, if someone loses their lease for their dancing studio or karate classes and so requests the use of church facilities to continue their business, their request would likely be turned down even though they offer to pay for the space. These are businesses rather than ministries. Requests for the use of space for political organizations are also turned down.

The Dream Team wants to say *Yes*, and says *Yes* far more times than it says *No*. Staff and members of the team work with people in the earliest stages of their discernment to help them prepare for presenting their ideas, sometimes meeting them beforehand to clarify or modify a proposal so that questions of mission can be addressed.

Questions about alignment run deep. Dream Team members consider, "Will this ministry multiply people and resources for ministry? Does it multiply impact, reach people we otherwise would not be able to reach, serve a human need, reduce suffering, address an injustice, or change lives? Will it really make a difference? What is the fruit in changed lives, and are these changes consistent with our mission in Christ?" The main role of the Dream Team is to multiply and deploy leaders for ministry.

Who Will Do It?

The second question the Dream Team addresses is, "Who takes responsibility for this program?" They want to know who will be the champions for this cause? Who has the passion, gifts, and time to make the program happen?

They ask presenters who else they have recruited to plan and lead the ministry, and who are the prospective participants or attendees.

Many denomination programs don't work in local churches because they don't begin with excited, passionate persons in the congregation who feel called, motivated, and gifted to lead them. No champions emerge from the congregation to buy into the programs with enough energy and enthusiasm to make them work.

A ministry needs a team of dedicated people committed to an idea in order for it to succeed. People can't merely bring good ideas expecting the pastor and staff to fulfill them. Expecting staff to do everything undermines the fundamental assumptions of lay ministry, the identification of spiritual gifts, and the calling of God for every person to serve. Those who lead a ministry must relate to the staff in a healthy and positive way, but they can't simply add to staff responsibilities. Because something is a good idea doesn't mean that the staff should make radical changes in their schedules and priorities. The pastor and staff offer support, encouragement, and counsel, but they shouldn't necessarily carry the portfolio of every ministry.

The Dream Team asks the presenter about the team they plan to build, the people who are already supportive, and how they plan to get more people engaged. If someone feels called to start a new class, they identify some of the people who are already committed to attend. Who are the core people? Who else is going to come? How will they be invited? Volunteers that plan a new class must draw people into their ministry and not expect the church or the pastor to push people into it.

How Will It Be Funded?

The third question the Dream Team asks is "How will the ministry be funded?" What's the plan for long-term sustainability? People are not allowed to dump their idea at the doorstep of the church, expecting the church to pay for it by adjusting the budget and defunding other ministries. The pastor and staff are not responsible for funding and will not round up people to make it work or stretch the budget to raise funds for it. As one Dream Team member says, "You can't expect someone else to do what God called you to do!"

Does the prospective ministry cost anything, and who bears those costs? Most ministries have no costs or are self-funded. Starting a Bible study or forming volunteers into a team to address a particular need may have no financial implications, outside of nursery care for children, and so financial questions are moot. Other ministries require gathering nominal fees to cover the costs of books, meals, or equipment. For ministries that require more funding, the Dream Team asks, "Have you identified people with the financial resources to make the ministry work?" You don't really have a ministry plan until you have a financial plan to support it.

For instance, a few people might step forward who feel called to form a team of first responders to represent the church following floods or tornados to clear trees, provide water, or help with search and rescue. They have their own pickup trucks, campers, and chainsaws. They are willing to receive training together from the conference office. As for funding? They plan to pay for the training themselves. They intend to travel together and room together to save costs. Or, they may present a plan to raise the money during the next two months. If they are forming the team at the request of the church, the church missions committee funds the training. A financial plan always undergirds the ministry plan.

Jeff Brinkman and Woods Chapel have used these permission-giving strategies for several years, and the ministries of the church have blossomed. More than 1,500 people regularly attend worship, and the church has become a leader in disaster response, missional engagement, and starting new faith communities.

"It makes such a difference to have lay leadership that learns to believe that *Yes* is a possibility, and that the principal task of leadership is to make things possible instead of thinking about why things can't work," Jeff says. "Much of this could have happened just by changing our brains and attitudes, but changing the structure also helped. Even in other operational committees, we stopped voting and moved to consensus. When a proposal is offered or a motion made, we say, 'Anyone see anything about this they can't live with?' If no one has major problems with it, we approve it."

Jeff distinguishes being in charge from being a leader. Being in charge has to do with control. Being a leader has to do with seeing that things happen, whether you are personally involved or not, and regardless of who receives credit.

One Well-Placed Yes

First United Methodist Church of Sedalia, Missouri, provides another example of a permission-giving church. In a community of 21,000 people, First Church's attendance has grown from 100 people to 950 over the last seventeen years under the leadership of Rev. Jim Downing.

Say Yes! To Life, to Love, to God is the motto at First Church, and it appears on their logo, website, and signage. They invite people to say *Yes* to God, *Yes* to serving, and *Yes* to ministry. For those who have no relationship with the church and are contemplating their first steps toward Christ, they say, "One well-placed *Yes* is a great place to start!"

The process by which new ideas emerge, find support, and come to fruition is similar to that of Woods Chapel, with minor differences in language and emphasis. The church considers the following questions when someone suggests an idea for ministry: Have you prayed about it? Do you believe it is God's will for us at this time? (Timing is important: do we have the right people, the right resources for sustainability, the right alignment with the priorities of the church for this ministry at this time?) Will it bring glory to Jesus Christ? (Or, are we just doing this because the church down the street is doing it?)

Jim believes God gives people ideas. Dreams and visions, as described in Acts 2, are part of following Christ. But people have to discern their participation in those ideas. Leaders and staff help people with their discernment. They pray with them and help them refine their ideas. As with Woods Chapel, First Church operates on the assumptions that everyone has spiritual gifts, everyone is called to ministry, and the work of the church is to help people grow in discipleship and in serving.

Many churches don't say *Yes* because they are afraid to fail. And yet growing churches try many things that don't work. Some things fail and other ministries require tweaking and modifying to make them work.

Jim tells members that God has already given them the green light for ministry and that they don't need permission. The Great Commission says "Go…" not "Stop…" *Say Yes!* is the church's way of telling people that you don't have to understand everything about God before following Jesus or trying ministry or taking the first step. Just as Martha said when Jesus asked her whether she believes. "Yes, Lord, I believe that you are the Christ, God's son" (John 11:25-27) sets life in motion, even if we don't have all the answers and can't see all the steps to come. One well-placed *Yes* is a great place to start!

An Anchor Habit

Woods Chapel and First Church in Sedalia exemplify the guided autonomy described in an earlier chapter. Laity and staff are encouraged to pursue their callings within the parameters set by the mission and priorities of the church. Those feeling called to lead or participate in a ministry do not feel abandoned; nor do they feel controlled. They feel encouraged and connected, set free and supported.

Lyle Schaller once observed that when it comes to initiating new ministries, congregations should "Count only the Yes votes."[2] By this he means, don't let those who have no interest in the new work veto those who have the energy and inspiration to do a project. Not everyone has to attend and participate in a project for it to be effective and life changing. Leaders don't have to promise their support to affirm new ministries; they merely have to withhold their disapproval. Let those who feel called and passionate make it happen. If five people want to form a Bible study, but twenty-five have no interest in it, just count the five and then get out of their way.

Churches that adopt missional assumptions change their habits to become more permission giving.

The idea of an anchor habit comes from the fitness world. People may have multiple goals that affect their physical well-being—to lose weight, eat better, get more exercise, reduce alcohol consumption, and get more sleep. Instead of focusing equally on all of these, they're encouraged to identify an anchor habit, a practice that, if done with utmost consistency, will affect all the other goals. The anchor habit might be rising early and running for a couple miles every day. People who develop this habit and complete it regularly discover that they eat better, moderate their weight, sleep better, and feel less drawn to excessive alcohol use. One anchor habit influences all the other behaviors that lead to the desired outcomes.

The same is true for the spiritual life. A common anchor habit is rising early for thirty minutes of prayer, devotional reading, or scripture study. A person who practices this habit regularly will be more inclined to attend worship, to pray at other times during the day, and to treat their family and coworkers with greater kindness and patience. They are more inclined to help others. They are more inclined to recognize God's calling and to respond. One single anchor habit helps shape their whole spiritual walk.

In a similar fashion, the creation of the Dream Team that met regularly to help people cultivate their callings into ministries had the effect of an anchor habit. The other committees necessary for the work of the church continued—finance, trustees, personnel. And all the basic frameworks of ministry remained—worship, pastoral care, children's ministries, service projects. But by naming a Dream Team, Woods Chapel assured that these various ministries remained fresh and open to experiments and innovations. By remaining faithful to this anchor habit, other positive habits become easier to maintain.

Better Systems

Even if a congregation chooses not to restructure or to add a Dream Team, it can improve its missional focus by re-evaluating leadership structures to make them more permission-giving, beginning with the principal governing board of a congregation, such as the Administrative Council.

The first task of leadership for the governing board is to focus the organization on its primary mission, to "cradle the vision" as some say. A leadership team defines, refines, extends, and limits the mission to unify all constituent components, to set direction and priority, and to mobilize people for work that contributes to the mission. Leaders hold ministry teams accountable for the mission and align resources for the task.

Second, *an effective leadership council pushes the whole organization to focus outwardly and presses leaders and staff to look to the needs of those they seek to serve.* Peter Drucker writes, "An organization begins to die the day it begins to operate for the benefit of the insiders and not the benefit of the outsiders."[3]

The church fulfills its mission at the margins of the congregation, where those who actively follow Christ encounter those who aren't a part of the community of faith. Remember the image of a congregation as concentric circles. In the center circle are the pastor, the leaders and staff, and key volunteers who plan and think and pray and act to lead the church. Farther out is the circle that includes other leaders, including teachers, volunteers, and helpers, and then another circle for those who attend and participate in worship, work projects, and Bible studies. The next larger circle includes all those who attend with less consistency.

When we reach the edge of the farthest circle, we discover on the other side of the margin the people who are not part of the community of faith. The church fulfills its mission at that edge, where those who belong to the community engage and interweave their lives with those outside the community. There, at the margin, we fulfill our mission, through *service and justice* ministries—helping, serving, relieving suffering—and through our *sharing the goods news of Christ*—seeking, inviting, welcoming, and nurturing faith. In a missional church, the boundary is wonderfully permeable, and members reach across the edge and new people easily enter into the faith community. The mission of the church isn't fulfilled in church planning meetings composed of church members talking with other members about church business, although those meetings may be important to strategize about the mission. The margin is where the action is.

Talkers become doers, and our mission in Christ becomes incarnate at the margins.

Jesus focused his attention on the margins of the community, usually over the objection of the religious leaders of his day and the counsel of his followers. Nearly every gospel story involves Jesus speaking with the marginalized: eating with tax collectors, healing lepers, engaging a woman at the well, interceding on behalf of a woman accused of adultery, receiving children, challenging moneychangers, praying with a thief on the cross. No stories tell of Jesus attending meetings! When he gathers his disciples, he draws their attention to the people at the margins: "I assure you that when you have done it for one of the least of these brothers and sisters of mine, you have done it for me" (Matt 25:40).

A critical role of leadership is to continually draw the attention of the church to the margins where the mission is fulfilled. Leading means outward-focused thinking. Who is our neighbor, locally and globally, and what does God call us to do? Effective leadership focuses on the needs and opportunities of the mission field.

Third, *a good leadership team forces future-oriented thinking.* It stays attuned to the culture, anticipates trends, notices threats, and focuses on sustainability. It watches trajectories, takes the long view on issues related to personnel and the use of resources and property, and evaluates the usefulness of strategies and operations. It helps the organization to change and adapt, to remain relevant and effective. An effective board refuses to avoid the difficult challenges. It thinks about next generations, fosters innovation, and assures long-term continuance of the mission.

Finally, *a governing board stays connected to its base, to those who elected its members and authorized their work.* It communicates with its constituencies and invites their participation in the mission. It can't become isolated from the people most invested, especially the laity, staff, and volunteers of the church.

Technically Elegant Administration

With the principal leadership team clear about its task, the next area to focus is the committee structure of the church. Is the work of the congregation organized in a way that supports the mission and work in the most effective manner? Most denominations require a few standing administrative committees, such as finance, trustees, and personnel, and then allow congregations to organize according to context, with additional teams, task forces, and committees. These should be formed carefully with attention to selecting the right people and working on the right tasks in the most technically elegant manner.

The words "technically elegant" may bring to mind the sleekest new mobile phone with the most fantastic features, but let's use it instead to describe better administration in a complex organization. What makes the organization of congregational leadership technically elegant?[4]

A technically elegant organizational system is user-friendly, intuitively understandable, simple, and effective. It solves numerous critical communication issues. It accomplishes the mission, and aligns personal, financial, and organizational resources.

A technically elegant system works smoothly for the people who participate in it rather than frustrating and exhausting them. It releases the talent and the ideas of people rather than restraining or stifling them. It provides the best conditions for people to offer themselves for leadership and to bear fruit.

In a technically elegant administrative system, people are clear about who does what, and they operate without undue territoriality or defensiveness. People know what resources are available to them and to whom they are accountable. People important for a decision aren't left out of the loop, and projects don't get stalled by an expectation of complete consensus.

All committees and staff have a direct line of sight between the work they do and the mission of the church and the ministry of Christ. They have a sense of where the congregation is going as a whole, and how their task fits into the larger picture.

Technically elegant systems connect people to work collaboratively on large objectives and minimize activities that are irrelevant, nonproductive, or unnecessary. They optimize organizational relationships. People work together who most need to do so, and teams are able to make decisions without excessive bureaucratic layers of permission seeking. Information flows efficiently and reaches those first who most need it to do their work. Technically elegant systems attract and select excellent leadership, people who are knowledgeable, talented, and effective in their area of expertise.

Such systems foster deliberate and thorough decision making in a timely manner so that the congregation remains agile enough to respond to opportunities quickly.

This describes an ideal, and no system works perfectly. And yet describing technical elegance gives us something to aim for.

Systems that say *Yes* result in permission-giving churches, which do the following:

They end the practice of holding useless meetings. Every person who leaves a meeting drives home knowing why the meeting was held and why their attendance mattered.

They hold fewer meetings with fewer people. At the same time, they offer more opportunities to serve in ministry for more people.

They cease being reporting organizations and become learning organizations. Pastors and leaders have to do a great deal of learning just to understand what the challenges are for their mission, and then they have to do even more learning to figure out steps forward.

They accept failure as a possibility. They aren't paralyzed by the fear of failure. They realize that some ministry initiatives don't work, or some require major adjustments to continue.

They work with clear expectations and high accountability.

They protect innovators and the fresh voices that want to do things in a different way.

A Sensible System to Get Things Done

The goal of rethinking congregational systems is to make them more accessible, sensible, and effective in accomplishing multiple ministries.

The designers of a university campus became concerned because students and faculty cut across lawns as they walked from one building to another instead of using the concrete sidewalks, resulting in well-worn dirt footpaths that ruined the landscaping. The paths developed as people naturally sought the shortest and most convenient route between buildings, but they made a mess of the landscaping. When the university built an additional complex of buildings, the designers decided not to plan sidewalks until after the buildings were in use. They waited until they saw where the footpaths formed, and then put the sidewalks in those places.

Similarly, instead of setting up an organizational structure and making everyone serve on the prescribed committees, a congregation can look at what is useful for its ministries and then establish teams, taskforces, and structures that support it. If a church has a significant program for feeding the homeless, it creates a team of people to give leadership to it. They invite a representative from the team to report occasionally to the administrative council when critical decisions arise. The same church may have trained disaster response teams. Again, a leadership team may coordinate the work and relate it to the larger church. The church may offer a contemporary worship service that requires weekly meetings of musicians, worship planners, pastors, and coordinators. This same church that has a team for the homeless ministry, for disaster response work, and for leading the worship service may not need a standing committee on missions or on worship as commonly prescribed. Maintaining committees that don't fit the ministry is like maintaining sidewalks where no one walks rather than constructing them along the pathways that make the most sense.

A Different Approach

Let's return to Dana, whose story is told in the opening of chapter 2, and her calling to form a team to respond after a tornado. In the earlier scenario, she carried her idea from committee to committee for eighteen months, and by that time the opportunity was lost.

Let's imagine a different scenario: This time, instead of referring her to a committee that meets months later, the pastor asks Dana to invite everyone she knows who shares her desire to do something to a meeting the following Tuesday. She encourages Dana to explore the costs of the training and the expenses of travel by contacting the denominational office or another church who has done similar work.

On Sunday, the pastor invites anyone else who feels called by God to help to come to the Tuesday meeting. Ten people show up, including Dana, a few of her friends, the pastor, and five people who responded to the announcement during worship.

Imagine the energy! These people are here because they share a common calling and a desire to help with a particular challenge. There's eagerness, enthusiasm, and passion. These folks talk one another into bolder action.

Dana tells them that two people will need training in order to lead the team, and three people volunteer. The project will require a pickup truck, a chain saw, and a variety of other equipment, and immediately people put forth ideas about where these can be found. She tells them that the cost is $2,000, and no one blinks an eye. They brainstorm about sources for the money. One person says his Sunday school class will help, another volunteers to talk to the women's group, and a third offers to contribute a couple hundred dollars.

Is it easier to raise $2,000 from ten people who are committed to a project or to change a church budget by $2,000? These ten people think of a hundred ways to raise the money because they are enthusiastic and called.

Later these ten people, led by Dana, take their plan to the church council, reporting that the money is already pledged and that ten people have volunteered to go. Another six people are providing food and supplies and five more have formed a prayer team to support them in their endeavor. They ask for the blessing of the church council, and everyone applauds and promises to support the work with their prayers. They're proud of the work their church is doing to help people.

This represents a different system, even though it involves the same people. The example illustrates the easiest and simplest shift a congregation can make to become more permission giving. People have been encouraged to make responsible contributions to the ministry of Christ without having to ask permission several times. The process has involved conversations by a variety of people who feel called rather than formal reports by a few elected leaders on a committee. A church that repeats this pattern increases the number of spiritually engaged laypersons. Rather than a few leaders meeting to focus on the business of the church, a larger number get involved in ministries that help them grow in discipleship while also making a difference in the world. A cumbersome, restraining system has been replaced by a permission-giving process that unleashes people for ministry. Systems can say *Yes*!

Sometimes *No* Is the Right Answer

Wikipedia is known for its open-source environment that invites and permits millions of users to contribute to its content. Wikipedia functions as a permission-giver by inviting anyone anywhere to submit information or update facts in its online encyclopedia. It's rooted and grounded in *Yes*! But even such a *Yes*-oriented entity as Wikipedia has its managers to protect value, quality, framework, and purpose. *No* is still important.

In order to accomplish the mission and to remain healthy and fruitful, permission-giving churches also adopt guidelines. Sometimes they say *No*. The following are legitimate reasons churches say *No*:

A ministry idea does not align with the mission, priorities, or spirit of the church. A person who says he feels called to teach classes at the church on photography, or sculpting, or golf would be told *No*, not because there's anything wrong with these activities but because they don't further the mission of the church. Someone who feels called to lead sessions on why God loves Christians more than Muslims, Jews, and Hindus would be told *No* because these ideas are not consistent with the theology and the spirit of the congregation.

This isn't the right time. Someone may feel called to organize a ministry that perfectly aligns with the mission and priorities of the church, enjoys enormous support, and has little or no financial impact, but nevertheless the time is simply not right to launch it. Perhaps the idea requires an expertise that no one has who currently belongs to the church or the church is immersed in another major initiative that would make focusing on something else impossible. Maybe the church is going through a transition of pastoral leadership or involved in a capital funds campaign. In all these cases, *No* really means *Not Now.*

The idea relies upon resources that the church doesn't have or which those who feel called cannot provide. Persons who say, "the church ought to" or "you people ought to" are missing the point of discerning gifts and callings. People can't dump ideas on the church expecting staff to do them and others to pay for them. Proposed ideas must have someone who is willing to say "I will" or "We will" rather than "The church ought to." Sustainability comes from sources and assets that people can identify at the outset.

The idea doesn't have champions to interpret and lead it and to rally people together. The initiative doesn't resonate with others or has no core group of called, passionate, gifted people to carry it forward. No one can make the church force people to attend something. For a ministry to be adopted, announced, and offered to others requires a core team or a group large enough to provide critical mass to lead and participate. A good idea without champions likely receives a *Not Now* rather than a *No*, and the church waits for the right mix of people to be called by God before returning to the idea.

The ministry idea significantly impacts the entire congregation and so requires wider conversation, greater consensus, more strategic planning, or considerable financial redirection. A few people who feel inspired to build a gym, launch ministry on a second campus, or add a worship service cannot proceed on their own and shouldn't receive a green light until much wider deliberation is held. These ideas require significant investment by the entire congregation. The answer cannot be *Yes* without further work, prayer, and planning, and any affirmation is merely for taking the next step in a lengthier process of preparation and communication.

The ministry is not one that can be done with excellence. A *Not Now* response might also be appropriate for a good idea that simply can't be offered with excellence because the church can't find the right leaders or resources at the time. Churches should never settle for mediocrity in launching initiatives.

A new worship service requires excellence in musical leadership and worship planning. A hands-on project to repair a bathroom or build a wheelchair ramp should not be offered unless there are a few experienced people on the team who understand carpentry and roofing.

Those seeking to lead a ministry refuse accountability. Anyone offering a ministry that will use the church's name, people, or facility should willingly invite and accept feedback, evaluation, assessment, and supervision. If a ministry doesn't meet agreed-upon participation benchmarks and financial support, remains unfruitful or doesn't fulfill its intended purpose, then the ministry should be ended.

The ministry is initiated for the wrong reasons. A ministry idea that is perceived by church leaders as self-serving, self-promoting, or merely for publicity should not receive approval. A ministry that is initiated for the purpose of competing with another program within the church cannot be supported. A ministry that is launched to undermine the authority of leaders or staff should not receive support.

Those seeking to start a ministry refuse to collaborate with others or to weave the ministry into the fabric of the church's other ministries. Those who insist that their work remains entirely independent and disconnected from core leadership cannot lead ministries of the church.

Activities are intended for personal profit. People who want to use church facilities for their personal for-profit business should be told *No*, including members who want to offer jewelry parties, karate classes, or investment seminars intended to recruit clients. The church is not a business and all activity should be non-profit.

The idea is brought by someone who displays spiritually or emotionally unhealthy patterns in their relationships. The pastor and leaders of the congregation have a responsibility to protect the well-being of the church and the people who participate in its ministries, and this may require making hard decisions related to personnel and volunteers. If people seek to initiate a ministry who are given to conflict, use intimidation, insist on their own way, have controlling personalities, treat people unkindly, or demonstrate an unhealthy defensiveness, leaders must find the courage to say *No* or to redirect such persons to supportive roles rather than to leadership. We cannot say *Yes* if it puts people at risk just because we're afraid of not being nice. Someone with a history of sexual misconduct, harassment, or other boundary issues cannot be given unmonitored access to vulnerable people. Neither can the church support someone with an ax to grind or who is driven by animosity toward the pastor. One pastor who leads a permission-giving church said, "We ask ourselves, 'Can this person play well with others?' We also consider how active the person is in his or her discipleship and growth in faith. Do they actively attend worship and support the church with their gifts? No one is entrusted with leadership who doesn't worship, give, and serve."

The ministry does not bear kingdom fruit. If a ministry is not bearing fruit, stop doing it. Closing down unfruitful work is difficult, but necessary. Peter Drucker said, "Practice planned abandonment." One of the most difficult elements of leadership is deciding what *not* to do. This involves learning to say *No* to the things that demand our time but which are not critical to our purpose so that we can say *Yes* to the things that are essential. Practicing planned abandonment means ending ministries that no longer bear fruit, are no longer sustainable, or which do not serve the present context. This is difficult for congregations to do. Congregations find it easier to start new ministries than to end unfruitful ones.

The Messiness of Yes

Yes can be dangerous. Unleashing people for ministry sets a church on an unpredictable path. It multiplies ministry. It interrupts business as usual. *Yes* unleashes the wild, raw nature of God. It changes people, and it changes the culture and momentum of a church. If you prefer a tightly controlled organization, then *Yes* is a mess.

The pastor of a church with dozens of ministries involving hundreds of volunteers was asked, "How do you control everything?" He answered, "I don't. It's like a herd of elephants that have been set loose: the idea isn't to stop them or control them, but to get them all running in the same general direction!"

Another pastor observed, "If every single thing that happens has to cross my desk for approval, then I become the limiting factor. That guarantees that we will remain small."

Congregations that operate with missional assumptions and that develop permission-giving systems require leaders that get out of the way, that encourage rather than control, and that release talent rather than stifle it. The shift in congregational culture cannot happen unless the pastor and critical leaders adopt a new leadership style. Change in the church begins with change in ourselves, and that brings us to the next chapter on leaders who say *Yes*.

Questions for Reflection and Discussion

1. How does a new idea move through your congregation from the initial conversations to actual ministry? How many steps are required to receive approval? Can you map the path from inspiration to fruition, from idea to outcome?

2. Do people initiating ministries feel encouraged or restrained by the governance systems of your church?

3. What helpful insights did you learn from the description of the Dream Team—a small group of elected laity and staff who receive ministry ideas—and the Three Questions used to discern and empower new ministries? How might these questions benefit your church's decision-making processes?

4. How does your congregation use a common language, such as a mission statement, to give direction to work? How well has the language taken hold?

5. The writer suggests that leaders end the practice of holding useless meetings. Is this suggestion relevant to your experience?

6. Why is it so hard for a church to decide to stop doing something that no longer works, or to stop doing something the way it has always been done?

7. Compare Dana's experience of organizing a disaster response ministry described in the opening pages of chapter 2 to the approach outlined in this chapter. What are the advantages and the risks of these two approaches?

8. The chapter describes several reasons to say *No* or *Not Now* in response to new ideas. Are there other reasons you would add?

To Delve Deeper

Explore Hebrews 11:1-8 from Eugene Peterson's *The Message,* which includes "By an act of faith, Abraham said yes to God's call to an unknown place." What Abraham and Sarah did sounds edgy, impulsive, dangerous, and a little reckless, and yet they are lifted up as models of faith. What do we learn about faith and about moving forward in this passage?

Prayer

Lord, we pray that in you we will break fresh ground in our thinking and doing. Help us imagine fresh ministries that are bold, relevant, and effective in fulfilling your callings for us. Place us in situations that cause us to change our minds and lead us to people that cause us to change our hearts. Help us dream dreams worthy of your calling. Open us to following you, even when that takes us to places we might never have chosen to go on our own volition.

Chapter Six

Leaders Who Say Yes!

Changing Attitudes and Behaviors

C ongregations and operational systems never become more permission-giving than the people who lead them. Leaders have a disproportionate influence on the culture and content of a church, and on the processes that either restrain or multiply ministries. They can discourage innovation, resist change, tighten rules, and ignore the gifts and callings of people. Or they can cultivate innovation and creativity and encourage people to discern and follow their callings to serve. Leaders foster openness to initiatives, or they squeeze people into the models of ministry they prefer. A willingness to let God change us and a desire to adapt our attitudes serve as prerequisites to lasting change. Permission-giving churches cannot thrive without permission-giving leaders.

Who? Me?

During my tenth year as pastor of a large multistaff church, the laity offered me a twelve-week study leave for rest, renewal, and learning. I was absent during the summer months as volunteers and staff planned the fall schedule. Upon my return, I discovered a program full of great new ministries—an eight-week lay academy that offered a dozen Bible studies and small group classes for adults, a Wednesday children's program that had been radically reinvented, a missions initiative that addressed an unmet need in the community using dozens of volunteers, the launching of a young couples class, and a new approach to using our projection screens in worship. All of these were departures from the usual programs that we had used successfully for years.

As I looked at the fall program, I thought, "These are great ideas. Why didn't we think of these things when I was there?" Then it dawned on me: maybe we didn't initiate these things before now *because* I had been there!

If I had been present during those months of planning, the fall program would likely have looked similar to that of previous years. While I think of myself as open to ideas and an encourager of experimentation, there are times when I'm the one whom God has to work around for accomplishing creative change.

Sometimes leaders are the obstacles to innovation without knowing it. Pastors and laypersons inadvertently interrupt imaginative and creative discernment. If I had been present when someone suggested starting a lay academy, I might have immediately asked for details—Who? What? Why? Where? What will it cost? These reasonable sounding questions, when those in authority ask them too early, have the effect of expressing doubt, of focusing on obstacles rather than on goals and desired outcomes. They cause people to yield too easily to what is practical and convenient. My body language might have shown my reluctance to invest the additional time and effort to try something different rather than to continue with what was familiar. My questions might have quashed the idea before it could begin to take hold.

It's hard work to delve deeply into what really needs to be done, and to permit the change that God is calling us to make. Questions of intention, of purpose, and of how best to fulfill the mission easily get pushed aside by notions of expedience and familiarity. We do what seems easiest and take the path of least resistance because doing what we really desire demands too much commitment or costs too much.

When God called Moses to return to Egypt to set the people of Israel free, he immediately interrupted God with several good excuses as to why this wouldn't work. Before Moses could absorb the complete vision God had for the future, he questioned how he could get people's attention, how he would get the people to follow him, and how he would be able to speak effectively. The huge, God-sized vision of setting free the people of Israel could have died if God had said, "Yes, Moses, these are problems. Let's postpone action until we eliminate the obstacles."

As I reflect on the signature ministries that characterize the churches I've served, many of them came to fruition over my initial objections, confusion, avoidance, or resistance. I had to be drawn into them, pulled and pushed and convinced. And no doubt many good things never came to fruition because somewhere early on, I was the obstacle.

Leading a permission-giving church requires becoming a permission-giving leader. Change in the church begins with the change in values, attitudes, and behaviors that takes place in us.

A Shift in Attitudes

Many leaders have become accustomed to the culture of *No*, and they have to change their leadership habits in order to cultivate a permission-giving environment. It's difficult to shift from being a *No* person to a *Just Say Yes* leader. Changing ourselves is the hardest task.

The *No* person looks for problems, and then focuses exclusively on how to fix them. The problem-finder's obsession with things that are broken sometimes has the effect of magnifying not merely the perception of the problem, but the problem itself.

"I serve a dysfunctional church," a pastor says. "I could never get my people to do that."

"That would never work here," a layperson laments. "Our church doesn't have enough people or money."

The repetition and reinforcement of these negative perceptions create a self-fulfilling prophecy. Leaders who focus exclusively on what's broken, what doesn't work, and what can't happen foster an environment that makes change impossible.

Permission-giving leaders rid themselves of the idea that the future is in someone else's hands, the direction of the congregation is beyond influencing, and there's nothing that can be done.

These leaders understand that something is already working well, or else the congregation wouldn't exist anymore. What is going well? What is worthy of fostering, replicating, learning from, and passing on? What ministries need to be fed, nurtured, and improved, and which need to be left alone? What if we assume that the church does have people with great ideas and deep passions, and that new work can begin and become fruitful?

What if we believed that we have exactly enough people and resources to fulfill the ministry God is calling us to today? We may not have the people and resources to do what another congregation is doing or what our congregation did when it was at the peak of its attendance, but we have what we need to do what God is calling us to do now. In a culture of *Yes*, leaders are purveyors of hope. They believe in new life, new birth, and resurrection. They believe that God is at work in the minds and hearts of people, and that God is preparing people for ministries they never imagined.

A culture of *Yes* expects people to have ideas, gifts, and callings. It amplifies what works and encourages the passions and callings that already exist but which may remain unseen or hidden from view.

Permission-giving leaders shift from "How can I change those people to get them to do what I want?" to "What are the changes I'm willing to make to unleash people for ministry?" They embody the change they want to see happen. This shift in attitude is an antidote to helplessness and paralysis.

The Permission-Giving Leader

Permission-giving leaders trust people. They have confidence that most people love Christ, desire the best for the church, and operate with the highest of motives, and they believe that people have capacities and gifts for ministry. They don't feel the need to control everyone or to know everything that happens in the church. They are willing to let planning and conversation and ministry take place in their absence. They want people to feel confidant and supported enough to try things on their own. They celebrate the self-generating, self-organizing quality of groups who share a common passion and calling. They develop an aptitude for identifying, affirming, and building on the strengths and capabilities of laypersons and staff members. They don't feel threatened by an idea simply because they didn't think of it themselves.

Permission-giving leaders trust that God is at work in people and processes, that God calls people, gives people gifts for ministry, inspires them with dreams and visions, and connects them with others who share their passions. They'd rather err on the side of setting people free for ministry than on the side of withholding permission. They'd rather say *Yes* to five ideas and discover that only three of them come to fruition than to supervise processes that consistently delay and restrain initiatives. Permission-giving leaders trust that God works even through chaos.

Permission-giving leaders are initiators. Most people don't think outside the box because there's so much inside the box to keep them busy—unhappy parishioners, staff conflicts, budgeting pressures, weekly sermon preparation, pastoral care. Permission-giving leaders nevertheless take time to pursue their dreams. They experiment. They are learners. They visit other churches, talk with other pastors, learn from the mistakes of others. They improve and adjust and adapt. They model trying new things. They follow Abraham, who by an act of faith "said yes to God's call to travel to an unknown place that would become his home" (Heb 11:8 *The Message*).

They shift from saying "you ought," and frequently say "I will." They never ask people to perform ministries they are not willing to do themselves. Instead of "the church ought to do something about literacy," they say, "I'm going to offer myself as a tutor." Instead of saying, "You people ought to be more open to Hispanic immigrants," they say, "I'm going to study Spanish and volunteer with an agency that works with Hispanic immigrants." Invitation works better than coercion, and responding to a calling stimulates others to respond as well. They lead by example.

Permission-giving leaders are responsible risk takers. Some initiatives fail, but these leaders try nevertheless. They sometimes risk more than others think is safe and dream larger than others think is practical. They know that the cost of never experimenting is higher than the cost of occasionally failing.

Permission-giving leaders grow their churches by multiplication and not just by addition. Rather than merely helping small groups or mission teams add more members, they encourage groups to start more groups and teams to train more teams and classes to launch additional classes. They empower people to lead. They invite people to teach. They equip people to serve. They've learned to appreciate the difference between "doing ministry" and "causing ministry to happen," and they develop systems to foster both.

Permission-giving leaders understand the importance of big strategies and long-term planning and broad participation for large projects such as buildings, staff expansion, the establishment of values, and the articulation of vision. But they also realize that forward movement mostly comes from incidental experimentation, incremental steps, the cumulative effect of dozens of small groups and teams and services. Growing churches are more likely to muddle their way forward than to decisively adopt a major course change. Most learning helps them take the next step rather than to lead a revolution, and most directional change takes place a few degrees at a time rather than with a complete turnaround. They count it as much a victory to change one hundred things by 1 percent as to change one thing by 100 percent.

Permission-giving leaders know how to listen. They listen to the ideas of people who are new and to those of long-standing members. They become very good at the basics of ministry—listening, encouraging, maintaining focus, keeping a sense of humor. And permission-giving leaders spend generous amounts of time with those who do not belong to the church, those who are new, and those who are young in the faith. Those who are closest to the mission field know best what is needed, and so leaders learn from those outside the church. They protect the voices of those who are edgy and nontraditional. They view newcomers as creative allies for change. They give permission to people others may feel reluctant to support. They help people at all stages of faith to listen to God, to discern their callings and to follow their passions.

Permission-giving leaders work with a minimum of defensiveness and territoriality. They invite feedback and improve systems. They don't care who gets credit. They don't feel the need to be the center of attention. They collaborate, communicate, and cooperate. They share everything they can.

Permission-giving leaders get out of the way. They offer as few obstacles as possible, and they celebrate when others take the lead. Some ministries they support from the center stage, and others they encourage from the sidelines. They give other people a chance to shine, and they thank people for what they do. They cheer people on. They generously share credit for successes and gracefully accept responsibility for failures and missteps. They are willing to apologize.

Permission-giving leaders hold high expectations. They value excellence. They never knowingly do anything that is not well done. They go the second mile and expect others to do the same. They are willing to be held accountable, and they expect accountability in every ministry. They refuse to settle for mediocrity.

Permission-giving leaders are clear about the mission and confident about the future. They repeat and interpret the mission of Christ throughout the church. They reinforce the critical priorities, practices, and values of the congregation. They pray without ceasing for the mission of the church, for the people who belong to the church, and for those the church is called to reach. They know why we do what we do, and why it matters.

Permission-giving leaders seldom say *No* when presented with a new idea. They ask questions that are helpful rather than discouraging. They suggest refinements and improvements. They clear a path forward.

However, permission-giving leaders know when to say *No* and are not afraid to do so. They know when to say *Not Now* when the time is not ripe for ministry that otherwise aligns with mission. They phase out ministries that no longer bear fruit in order to redirect resources toward more fruitful ministries.

Permission-giving leaders set high-performing staff and volunteers free, entrust them with more responsibilities, and offer them more opportunities. They get out of their way. And permission-giving leaders give staff and volunteers that are performing moderately well the time and motivation to improve. They equip them for success by helping them grow and become more effective. For low-performing staff and volunteers, they establish clear expectations, solid deadlines, and clear consequences. They are willing to hold tough conversations with people who are ineffective and to close ministries that are unfruitful.

Permission-giving leaders know that exercising too much control limits the creativity and capacity of staff and volunteers. And they know the risk of abandonment, of giving staff and volunteers no guidelines or little support, or of operating with unclear expectations. They strike a balance that gives enough guidance to offer direction and support while offering enough autonomy that people can exercise their own creativity.

Permission-giving leaders work with flexible job descriptions in their supervision of others, seeing that the essentials are done well and giving space for people to follow their callings, explore ideas they are curious about, and experiment with new approaches. They act as a buffer to shield people from criticism who take responsible risks.

Permission-giving leaders never go it alone. They engage others, seek counsel, learn from others, form teams, seek out mentors, invite conversation, ask what others think, and develop feedback systems for testing new ideas.

Permission-giving leaders open options rather than close them. They widen possibilities rather than narrow them. They nudge people rather than nag them, inspiring and giving heart to those who are unsure. They operate with a both/and attitude rather than forcing either/or choices. They focus on the future. They instill a sense of hope.

Permission-giving leaders have the ability to say *Yes* even to people who think differently than they do about issues. They are gracious with those with whom they disagree. They do not insist on their own way. They do not demand uniformity. They protect the leadership offered by outliers and innovators. Permission-giving leaders enjoy seeing people thrive in their discipleship. They take satisfaction in the experiments, successes, and fruit of others.

Permission-giving leaders develop habits that keep them freshly engaged with young people, new people, visitors, and those who do not yet belong to the church.

Permission-giving leaders value the initiatives of laity as well as of pastors, staff, or committee members. They give people license to pursue their callings.

Innovation and Imagination

Organizations that are tightly organized, with a top-down flow of information, a controlling leadership, and heavy-laden with rules and multistep permission-seeking processes, are hard to change and resistant to innovation. Young people in particular find such organizations unnatural and unworkable, and they migrate toward more flexible structures. The tightness of the structure and the lack of flexibility become too much, and participants yearn for an organizational style that is less paralyzing and more agile, responsive, and resilient. They long for freedom, innovation, and creativity.

On the other hand, organizations that are too loosely organized become unfocused and chaotic with unclear expectations, unknown boundaries, and unstated purposes. Participants feel adrift, and they yearn for direction, clarity, alignment, accountability, and coordination.

When churches operate under too tight a structure, they long for more flexibility, and when they lack cohesive operations, they desire more consistency. Some swing back and forth between periods marked by an unhealthy controlling centralization and an unhelpful state of chaos.

During a time of paralysis in the church, John Wesley and the early Methodists experimented with innovations to reach people using methods that shattered expected approaches. Some elements of the Methodist movement were wildly chaotic, and others were characterized as disciplined and highly methodized. A little chaos proved to be good for the mission of the church, and an element of discipline also helped.

We are so keenly aware of how "methodized" we are today, with our rules, policies, structures, and disciplines, that we overlook the bold originality that characterized the early Methodists and other reform movements. Methodism began as a wildly creative experiment, risky and countercultural. Wesley's notions of forming classes, bands, and societies; of founding preaching houses and schools; of inner holiness and outward witness; of mobilizing people to visit the imprisoned and feed the poor; of field preaching and ordaining pastors for America—these experiments derived from an expansive and adventuresome sense of God's grace. Early Methodism was outward-focused and future-oriented, innovative and energetic.

Mainline pastors today operate in denominational systems and with congregational structures that are constraining. *Yes* is counter-cultural in mainline denominations. When connectionalism demands too much uniformity, we allow it to become a liability rather than a strength.

In a similar spirit as our forbearers, leaders must evolve from "What shall we do?" to "What shall we try?" and "What do we need to learn?" We have to encourage bold experimentation and learn from each other.

Marissa Mayer, when she served as vice president at Google, outlines various principles of innovation, and several are relevant for churches.[1]

First, she suggests ***ideas come from everywhere***. Ideas come from the top and also from the bottom, from the center and from the margins, from laity as well as pastors, from other congregations, from other denominations, and from corporations. Expect people to have ideas, and provide systems so that people can contribute ideas, sort through them, and experiment. People need permission to try things—launch ministries, start small groups, reach new communities, serve unmet needs.

Second, Mayer says **work with gifted people**. Convening conversations with highly talented laity and drawing them into the task of addressing key challenges accelerates innovation. Gifted people are focused on the cutting edge, constantly learning, given to experimentation, and asking for more opportunity. They are proactive. They are leaders in their communities, schools, and businesses and doing all kinds of work in the world, and they desire to do more than sit in the pew or serve on the finance committee. They yearn to use their gifts to make a difference.

A third principle of innovation is to **share everything you can**. Learning and leadership do not come only from the top. Laypersons learn from laity, churches learn from other churches. New ideas and best practices spread through networks with a minimum of territoriality. Permission-giving churches learn from other churches. They send laypersons and pastors to visit other congregations to see how they work, and they invite people who lead ministries in other congregations to come teach them how. When they discover an approach that works, they offer to teach others. They give away as much as possible.

Fourth, Marissa Mayer suggests that leaders **give people license to pursue their dreams**. Rather than expecting everyone to use the template of "this is how we always do it," instead they give them permission to use their passions and creativity to explore new ways. Leaders and staff have to feel the freedom, to give the permission, and to try bold new things without fear of failure.

Fifth, Mayer reminds us that **innovation does not mean instant perfection**. Experiments by their very definition do not always turn out as planned. Some initiatives never find traction, and some plans have to change so radically that they take a form no one ever anticipated. Innovation requires feedback that allows for quick adjustments, and the best projects require little corrections every day. Without failure-tolerant leaders, pastors won't feel free to experiment.

A sixth principle is that **creativity loves constraints**. Every project works within limits set by purpose, values, money, time, people, and context. Constraints sharpen clarity and focus resources. A stream with no banks has neither direction nor movement.

Permission giving does not mean everything goes. There are standards and expectations, accountability and collaboration, feedback and evaluation. A more open system does not mean a system that is easy or unaccountable.

In Marissa Mayer's world of technology, another principle is simply *users, users, users*, calling innovators to put the experience of the customer first.

In our context, the principle might be ***mission field, mission field, mission field***. Innovation requires constant attention to those God has entrusted us to serve. Innovation demands an outward focus, a missional purpose. We focus on the unmet needs and unreached people around us.

What are the best decisions you ever made as a leader? What are the best decisions your congregation ever made? Was it to try something? To risk something? To initiate something? An environment of innovation is imperative for reaching creative and new decisions.

Are innovation and initiative encouraged and rewarded, or restrained and subdued by our systems and attitudes?

Doing Less, Well

According to a well-known business leader, organizations should focus on doing less, well.[2] Organizations can pursue too many goals, adopt too many priorities, and sustain too many programs. Better to do a few things well than to do many things in a mediocre fashion. Instead of making an inch of progress on each of a hundred initiatives, it's better to make significant progress on the few most important ones. Sometimes less is more.

This seems to contradict a permission-giving model that sets people free in self-generating groups. But it's possible for such groups to work on widely different projects while still operating with the same values—doing work that is Christ-centered and operates with a premium on fruitfulness, excellence, accountability and collaboration—and that function under the umbrella of a common mission statement.

Some congregational practices are essential for the mission, such as offering quality worship experiences; creating a signature mission program that changes lives; providing a system for inviting, welcoming, and assimilating people; establishing small groups by which people grow in discipleship; and assuring programs that help people care for the sick, homebound, and bereaved. Every congregation must continually improve upon these core competencies. In a *doing less, well* church, these must be done with excellence. Within these core competencies, there is room for many ideas and innovations, approaches and programs. A culture of innovation is no contradiction to a focused organization with clear priorities.

In addition, ancillary ministries contribute to the mission even when they are not essential in themselves. They contribute to core competencies. An Alzheimer's support group or a Twins and More program never rises to the level of priority that worship holds. The fact that worship is more critical to a congregation's life shouldn't restrain those who feel called to offer these other ministries. Just say *Yes*. Focus, discipline, priority, and strategy are not incongruous with innovation, experimentation, and the encouragement of diverse expressions of ministry. A *doing less, well* strategy complements rather than competes with a permission-giving environment.

The Upside-Down Pyramid

Most people imagine the administration of the church as a pyramid, with the pastor on top; a few leading laypersons and staff a step below; the leaders of teams, chairpersons of committees, and teachers of classes just below that; the members of committees and participants on teams below that, and so forth.

The pyramid metaphor answers who's in charge and who's in control. Information, ideas, and decisions flow from the top down to the bottom. Positions are fixed and inflexible. There's a clear chain of command. Some serve in inferior positions and some lead from superior positions in a hierarchical fashion.

In a pyramid, every one carries the weight of the person above them, and of the persons above the person above them, until there's so much heaviness that the people on bottom can hardly move. Churches that consider themselves organized this way assume that they've designed an organization where information cascades perfectly from top to bottom so that everyone knows what to do and feels perfectly happy with the assignment. Is that really how churches work? A tightly controlled, centralized model seldom helps churches flourish, and it restrains the callings of people to serve Christ in a manner that uses their spiritual gifts.

Imagine a different metaphor. Imagine an upside-down pyramid, with the pastors at the bottom. The pastors see their task to undergird, support, and provide what is necessary for the staff and lead volunteers to do their work and offer their ministry. In turn, the staff and lead volunteers understand that their ministry is to provide the foundation and equipping and training and leading that helps other persons to serve, grow, and lead. They offer encouragement, training, support, and help. Each level helps and supports those above them to respond to God more faithfully and fruitfully. These people in turn see it as their task to discover their callings, use their spiritual gifts, and make a difference in the world for Christ in their daily lives and through ministries of serving. With each new level, there's a multiplying effect until hundreds of people are sent out into the world as ambassadors for Christ.

Or imagine the metaphor of a tree. The roots are our relationship with Christ, a clear mission statement, agreed upon values, and a vision for the unique ministry of this congregation. The trunk may be critical ministries that every church must perform well—worship, evangelism, mission, discipleship, and stewardship. The trunk provides the flow of spiritual, personal, and material resources that the branches require for fruitfulness. The branches might be the ministries that people form in response to God's call. New branches sprout with each season. Some branches complete their life cycle and are trimmed away. And on every branch there is the fruit of changed lives, the difference made for the purposes of Christ for those within the church and those far beyond the church. The tree—roots, trunk, branches, leaves, and fruit—is alive, growing, branching out. And within the fruit are the seeds of future trees.[3]

Abandon the standard pyramid. Pyramids are remnants of ancient civilizations. They are stone tombs. They are administrative, delivering decisions from on high rather than living, growing, life-giving, and fruitful. Permission-giving leaders do not impose their values and vision on the organization. Instead, they help discover, articulate, and live out the values, beliefs, and vision of the congregation. They undergird and support ministry, and they nurture the flow of spiritual gifts and callings into fruitful ministry.

Find an image that works for you. Expand the imagination of your church. Adopt a metaphor that makes it clear that it's not about us, that pastors and lay leaders are not on top, not at the center, and not in control. Everything doesn't depend upon centralized committees or hired staff. Adopt a model that shows that the real work of leadership is to help others exercise and develop their ministries as they grow in Christ. The focus is not on maintaining the church but on how the church and its people can be leaven in the community and become the salt of the world. Use a metaphor that reminds leaders to loosen up rather than to tighten down, to support and feed rather than to withhold permission, and to value freedom, choice, passion, and calling.

The Failure-Tolerant Leader

During a championship football game between two teams that were known for their careful, conservative, and consistent play, the TV commentator said, "I think that the team that makes the most mistakes is going to win."

The commentator was suggesting the team that breaks their usual pattern and takes more risks, and therefore makes more mistakes, would likely win over the team that played conservatively and predictably.

Or we can use an analogy from tennis, where players usually give their maximum effort on the first serve, knowing that if they fault on that one, they will have another opportunity. On the second serve, players usually take a more conservative approach to avoid getting a double fault.

Imagine a tennis player who determines never to double fault on the serve. He or she will serve so carefully that the opponent gains all the advantages. Fear of making the mistake will cause the player to lob easy serves that can be returned with overwhelming power. Playing too conservatively and too predictably never succeeds.

In a similar way, the fear of failure causes pastors and leaders to err on the side of safety, predictability, and restraint. Fear of failure paralyzes leaders. Fear blocks imagination. Permission-giving leaders have to overcome these fears to cultivate a culture of innovation and imagination. They must learn how to fail successfully.

Today congregations must take more risks in order to see fruitful results than congregations did in the past. Churches fifty years ago could remain strong, and even see growth, by offering one Sunday morning worship service with one style of music, good pastoral care, a youth ministry, and a solid administrative structure. The culture pushed people toward churches, and a passive stance worked. To be successful, churches just had to do what other churches were doing.

For churches to experience above-average results today means taking risks that average congregations, which are mostly growing older and getting smaller, are unwilling to take. Leaders have to dare to be different. They have to dare to be wrong.

Fruitful congregations thrive with an abundance of ministries, open the doors to new ideas, and take initiative to start ministries. Yet, fruitful congregations can list dozens of programs and initiatives that didn't work, failed to take root, lasted for a little while and faded away, or never bore the fruit that was hoped for. Growing congregations experience failure with more frequency than do declining congregations for the simple reason that they try more ideas than declining congregations. Even with all their failures, they never become failure averse in a way that keeps them from trying again. They remain resilient. They learn from their mistakes. They move on.

All congregations encounter obstacles, setbacks, and challenges. Perhaps a youth ministry declines precipitously. Maybe a staff member becomes ineffective or instills conflict. Some congregations avoid, deny, and ignore the challenge. They let it go unaddressed. Programs end. Ministry is diminished. People leave. The church's capacity to reach people decreases. Worry wins. The ministry of Christ loses. The congregation fails to learn what it needs to learn to move forward through the setback. With each challenge, the congregation shrinks a little more, withdraws back into itself, and becomes a little smaller.

Other congregations face the same challenge, but they do so with a sense of resilience and purpose. The pastor consults other pastors who face a similar setback. Leaders visit with leaders from other churches. They invite the help of a consultant. They read and attend workshops on the topic. They learn about the roots of the challenge, and then they learn approaches to take. They make decisions and take action. They try. And they come out on the other side of the challenge as a stronger church, a learning church, a more confident church that is clearer about its mission and more committed to its future. The church grows. They fail successfully.

Jesus tells the story of the master who entrusts his servants with various quantities of talents while he is away. The servant who receives ten talents returns ten talents more to his master upon his return, and the servant who receives five returns five more than he'd been given. However, the servant who received one talent dug a hole and hid it for fear of losing it, and for this he faced his master's disappointment. His fear paralyzed him into inaction.

Pastors and leaders have been entrusted with enormous responsibilities and with a mission given us in Christ. Leading requires humility and courage.

Leading requires the humility to get out of the way, to relinquish control, to trust others, and to trust how God works through others. Leading also requires the audacity, boldness, resilience, and fearlessness to try and try again, even when faced with failure, setback, and resistance. There is always a next step, no matter how difficult the challenge or how intransigent the system, and the most important decision is always the next one.

Questions for Reflection and Discussion

1. When was a time that you discovered that you were an obstacle to change and fresh ideas? How did you become aware of it? How has this awareness changed you?

2. Think of someone who exhibits the qualities of a permission-giving leader. What behaviors in yourself would you need to work on to become more permission-giving?

3. What are some of the most visible fruits of your personal ministry? How has God used you to change the lives of other people?

4. Which of the principles of innovation, if adopted and practiced consistently, would have the greatest positive impact on your church?

5. When did a ministry idea fail in your congregation, and what did you learn from it? How does knowing that even successful churches fail, help you become a more failure-tolerant leader?

To Delve Deeper

Read Luke 9:1-6 and 10:1-17 in the Common English Bible or the New Revised Standard Version. Now read these passages again using *The Message*, a translation by Eugene Peterson. How does your congregation send people into the mission field that surrounds your church? Do members feel "sent" in their daily lives? How do the leaders and members of your church learn to become more missional, intentional, and invitational in their personal ministries?

Prayer

Ripen in us the expectation of serving you fruitfully. Save us from arrogant self-congratulations, and help us honestly seek to view our ministry through your eyes. Help us never to grow weary or discouraged in seeking to love others as you have loved us, even when we cannot see the signs of change we hope for. Help us help our congregation to focus outward toward the mission field you have prepared for us in our own community, and to reach the people you have uniquely prepared us to reach. May your love become real in us, and your kingdom become visible through us.

Epilogue

The Ministry of Encouragement

O n May 22, 2011, a Force 5 tornado struck Joplin, Missouri, killing 162 people, injuring hundreds more, and destroying 8,400 homes, businesses, schools, churches, and hospitals. As bishop of the Missouri Area, I arrived as soon as possible and returned numerous times to offer prayers, consolation, and support to community members, first responders, and volunteers. From the day the storm hit and continuing for months, churches throughout the city, the state, and from across the nation mobilized for ministry. Congregations of all sizes and types—rural, urban, and suburban—responded with generosity, compassion, self-sacrifice, and creativity. They offered ministries they had never before imagined offering and initiated projects to rebuild homes, rebuild lives, and rebuild a community. Some responses were self-forming while most were coordinated with other churches, service organizations, and government agencies to maximize impact. The surge of ministry and generosity was overwhelming, heartening, and effective. Churches responded to human need and to God's call with a resounding, repeated, and persistent *Yes!*

A similar response followed the tragic shooting in Ferguson, Missouri, of an unarmed eighteen-year-old black man by a white police officer, an incident that brought to the surface racial tensions that had existed for years and that led to a sustained period of protests in 2014. Pastors, laypersons, and congregations exhibited extraordinary courage, initiative, compassion, and self-sacrifice as they offered a witness for peace, provided places of safety and respite during turbulent times, ministered to the children of Ferguson, helped with clean up, and set to work to address long-term issues of racism, profiling, mistrust of authority, underemployment, inequalities in the justice system, and the underrepresentation of ethnic officers in law enforcement.

In both Joplin and Ferguson, the *Yes* from churches was immediate and generous, creative and compassionate, and focused on the real needs of people. Congregations felt called by God to respond, and did so with courage and commitment.

109

When we contrast how congregations respond to crises and natural disasters with how they function in their daily operations, we notice a contradiction. In the face of overwhelming and immediate human suffering, congregations say *Yes* without hesitation, they do whatever it takes to provide assistance, and they respond quickly and effectively. Present a congregation with raw human need, and no one argues over meeting times, no one worries about reports, and no one demands a hundred steps of permission-seeking. Instead, people say, "you can count on us."

Yet in the usual course of operations, most congregations are slow, unresponsive, preoccupied with their own internal issues, restrained, and unfocused. The sense of imperative that sharpens in the face of urgent need remains mostly unseen during ordinary times.

A second contradiction in congregations is the noticeable contrast between the large number of ideas, passions, and callings among church members as compared to the small number of new ministries offered by a church. The imagination and commitment people bring to the task of discipleship feed ideas that lead to fruitful outcomes far less frequently than one would expect. Something dampens the spirit and makes people reluctant to offer themselves or their ideas in the ordinary course of church operations.

And yet a third contradiction is seen in how congregations publicly celebrate and invite creative ideas while systematically restraining, resisting, and covertly subverting those same ideas. Congregations yearn for gifted and energetic pastors, and then stifle every attempt their pastors make to lead. Churches lift up experienced and passionate laypersons to leadership, and then limit their capacity to try anything new. Under these restrictions, leading a congregation feels like driving a car with the parking brake on.

In the Sermon on the Mount, Jesus says to his followers, "You are the light of the world. A city on top of a hill can't be hidden. Neither do people light a lamp and put it under a basket. Instead, they put it on top of a lampstand, and it shines on all who are in the house. In the same way, let your light shine before people, so they can see the good things you do and praise your Father who is in heaven" (Matt 5:14-16).

These contradictions, unless they are resolved, have the effect of keeping a lid on ministry, shutting down capacities, and hiding the good news of Christ under a basket where no one can see its light.

The fact that congregations respond so quickly and effectively, mobilize people so well, and act with such agility during crises demonstrates that they are capable of courageous, compassionate, and life-changing ministry. The challenge is how to transfuse that experience into the ordinary practice of ministry.

Resolving the contradictions begins with a simple first step: *Just Say Yes!*

What if we could recover the sense of urgency and clarity about our mission in our daily operations that we see when congregations respond to natural disasters and emergencies? What if we could identify and cultivate more of the callings and use more of the spiritual gifts present in every congregation? What if we could celebrate creative initiatives without slamming on the brakes before new ministry ideas gain traction?

Imagine the unlimited and surprising ways God can use a congregation composed of people equipped and unleashed to do ministry anywhere, anytime. Imagine a church where people take the words attributed to John Wesley to heart: "Do all the good you can. By all the means you can. In all the ways you can. In all the places you can. At all the times you can. To all the people you can. As long as ever you can."

Imagine a church with a clear and robust mission, reinforced through preaching, teaching, mentoring, leadership training, and witnessing in worship, small groups, and teams.

Imagine leaders who realize that the most exciting thing about belonging to a church is doing ministry, not serving on a committee. Imagine a church that attracts people who are energetic and ready to serve rather than people infatuated by rules.

Imagine a congregation that goes to the places Christ would go and engages the people Christ would engage.

Imagine a congregation that operates less like a machine, with multiple-step, linear processes communicated through endless charts and boxes and rules, and more like a garden that is cultivated with love and care and attention.

Good ideas are not hiding, waiting to be found. Spiritual gifts are not in short supply. Altruistic impulses are not lacking in our people. Churches have to cultivate the right environment for these to become visible.

Cultivating an Environment of Yes

The image of a congregation as a garden draws our attention to the environment that surrounds ministry. Are conditions conducive to vitality, growth, and fruitfulness? Do seeds have enough moisture and proper soil to sprout, and are the conditions of light and nourishment right to grow into hearty plants that bring forth a harvest? Is our patch of earth free enough of rocks and weeds and other obstacles so that new life can take root? In such a model, growth never ends and everything is interactive—pastors, staff, lay leaders, work teams, volunteers, members, newcomers, youth, organizational processes—all contribute to favorable and fruitful outcomes. Everyone feeds ministry by recognizing gifts, fostering the call, nourishing new ideas, encouraging one another, and celebrating fruitfulness.

In a garden, growth takes time, patience, persistence, and care. You can do everything correctly and still experience failure. But when the conditions are right, something comes forth that never existed before.

Imagine creating an environment that fosters creativity, relies upon the encouragement of leaders, and is fed by the prayers of everyone. In such a place, the Spirit of God works in ways visible and invisible, and results come to fruition in tangible form through lives changed by Christ.

Scripture uses countless metaphors related to planting, harvest, seeds, sowing, vines, branches, farmers, and fruit. We cannot *make* a plant grow, but we can provide an environment that radically increases the prospects of a bountiful harvest. That's how permission-giving churches, systems, and leaders work.

The most direct and personal way to contribute to a permission-giving environment is through offering the ministry of encouragement.

Freshly released from slavery to the law to new life in Christ, the Apostle Paul writes about the law and the Spirit, "because what is written kills, but the Spirit gives life," (II Cor 3:6), and he associates the Lord with freedom, "The Lord is the Spirit, and where the Lord's Spirit is, there is freedom" (3:17). We serve a permission-giving God. By grace we experience freedom—not freedom to do as we please or to insist on our own way, but to offer ourselves fully, completely, and passionately to God, free from fear, free from guilt, free to love.

In light of this freedom, Paul repeatedly uses the language of encouragement. He instructs the Thessalonians to encourage one another and to build each other up (I Thess 5:11). Christians sometimes misunderstand encouragement as something shallow and mushy, repeating empty phrases about how positive everything will turn out. Or they offer encouragement that is so general, unspecific, and indiscriminate that it leads to unintended and unwanted consequences. Yet true encouragement involves something more profound. It steels people against despair. It emboldens them in their following of Christ.

Encouragement comes from the word *courage*, which derives from the French word for *heart*. *Encouragement* literally means "to fill with courage and strength of purpose, to hearten, to give heart." Encouragement refers to the action of giving someone support, confidence, and hope. To encourage is to inspire and motivate. Encouragement involves an element of gentle persuasion, of prodding, prompting, and urging. Encouragement emboldens rather

112

than restrains, empowers rather than limits, stimulates people to move forward rather than to retreat. Encouragement makes people more determined. It fortifies and instills resolve. Real encouragement means giving someone the strength to change. It confirms people in their callings and in their ministries.

What do we offer the person who is new to the faith and struggling to understand the life and teachings of Christ? Encouragement. The person who is curious about the spiritual life and feeling uncertain about how to pray? Encouragement. The person motivated to offer themselves as a volunteer for the first time? Encouragement. The person who wants to help strangers rebuild their homes or to help the homeless find food and shelter? Encouragement. The pastor who faces resistance and feels like giving up? Encouragement. People discerning their spiritual gifts, wrestling with a call to ministry, searching for God's intention for their lives? Encouragement. The person excited about starting a class or launching a children's ministry? Encouragement. Encouragement means giving someone the strength to change and grow and serve. Real encouragement means helping people say *Yes* to God.

Imagine a congregation where leaders take seriously the ministry of encouragement. This causes them to rethink how they regard newcomers, how they listen for ideas, how they evaluate their systems to become more permission giving. A ministry of encouragement shifts the focus about leadership from a pure programmatic, structural conversation to the larger issues of purpose and mission, helping people grow in discipleship and fulfill their callings. We serve a God that sets people free, invites people along, encourages them to try, calls them to serve, and sends them forth with blessing and assurance.

Systems can say *Yes*. People can adopt more open attitudes. Churches can cultivate the callings of their people and become better at identifying spiritual gifts. Leaders can create a permission-giving environment. Unleashing people for ministry begins with the simple task of encouraging one another and building one another up. *Just Say Yes!*

Notes

Chapter One: You Can't Do It That Way: People Who Say *No*

1. Ronald A. Heifetz and Marty Linsky, *Leadership on the Line: Staying Alive Through the Dangers of Leadership* (Boston: Harvard Business School Press, 2002), 26–30.

2. William Bridges, *Managing Transitions: Making the Most of Change* (Philadelphia: Da Capo Press, 3rd ed., 2009).

Chapter Two: Committees, Rules, and Policies: Systems That Say *No*

1. Jim Collins, *Good to Great and the Social Sector: A Monograph to Accompany Good to Great* (Boulder, CO: Jim Collins, 2005).

2. Ibid., 10.

3. Gordon MacKenzie, *Orbiting the Giant Hairball: A Corporate Fool's Guide to Surviving with Grace* (New York: Viking Penguin, 1998).

4. Peter Block, *The Answer to How Is Yes: Acting On What Matters* (San Francisco: Berrett-Koehler Publishers, Inc., 2002), 1.

5. I'm indebted to Marty Linsky, coauthor of *Leadership Without Easy Answers*, for this exercise, which he used in a seminar at a bishops retreat, St. Simons, GA, 2014.

6. Linsky seminar.

7. Linsky seminar.

8. Thomas L. Friedman, *The World Is Flat: A Brief History of the Twenty-first Century* (New York: Farrar, Straus, and Giroux, 2005), 318–21.

9. David Kinnaman and Gabe Lyons, *UnChristian: What a New Generation Really Thinks about Christianity, and Why It Matters* (Grand Rapids, MI: Baker Books, 2007), 28–29.

10. See chapter 2 of Thomas L. Friedman, *The World Is Flat: A Brief History of the Twenty-first Century* (New York: Farrar, Straus, and Giroux, 2005).

Chapter Three: Buildings, Bulletins, and Attitudes: Churches That Say *No*

1. See chapter 3 of Lovett Weems and Tom Berlin, *Bearing Fruit: Ministry with Real Results* (Nashville: Abingdon Press, 2011).

2. Adam Hamilton, *Leading Beyond the Walls: Developing Congregations With a Heart for the Unchurched* (Nashville: Abingdon, 2002), 21.

3. Ronald A. Heifetz and Marty Linsky, *Leadership on the Line: Staying Alive Through the Dangers of Leadership* (Boston: Harvard Business School Press, 2002), 27.

Chapter Four: Churches That Say *Yes!* Changing Fundamental Assumptions

1. Frederick Buechner, *Wishful Thinking* (HarperSanFrancisco, 1993, rev. and exp. ed.), 119.

2. This particular definition of discipleship derives from the General Rule of Discipleship used by Covenant Discipleship Groups. See Davis Lowes Watson, *Forming Christian Disciples* (Nashville: Discipleship Resources, 1991), 9.

3. Adam Hamilton is the pastor who whimsically described this shorthand way of thinking about discipleship and the attendant risks of self-referential pride.

4. Several of these examples of laypersons discovering their calling were originally shared in the book *Five Practices of Fruitful Living*, Abingdon Press, 2010.

Chapter Five: Systems That Say *Yes!* Becoming a Permission-Giving Church

1. The consultant was from Easum, Bandy, and Associates. Both William Easum and Thomas Bandy have written extensively about permission-giving congregations and leadership styles in such books as *Sacred Cows Make Gourmet Burgers* by Bill Easum and *Christian Chaos* by Tom Bandy.

2. Lyle E. Schaller, *Strategies for Change* (Nashville: Abingdon Press, 1993), 102.

3. "Important Lessons from Peter Drucker" in *Netfax*, July 7, 1997, a newsletter from Leadership Network, Tyler, Texas.

4. The words "technically elegant" to describe the goal of organizational alignment are from Franklyn Covey Company's *The 4 Roles of Leadership*, a seminar for leaders, 1999.

Chapter Six: Leaders Who Say *Yes!* Changing Attitudes and Behaviors

1. Several YouTube videos capture Marissa Mayer presenting the nine principles to various audiences, or search "Marissa Mayer's 9 Principles of Innovation." A summary by Chuck Salter can be found at http://www.fastcompany.com/702926/marissa-mayers-9-principles-innovation.

2. For a thorough discussion of the idea of "doing less, well," see *Essentialism: The Disciplined Pursuit of Less* by Greg McKeown (New York: Crown Business, a Division of Crown Publishing, 2014).

3. Gordon MacKenzie elaborates on the contrast between the pyramid and tree metaphors for organizations in chapter 18 of *Orbiting the Giant Hairball: A Corporate Fool's Guide to Surviving with Grace* (New York: Viking Penguin, 1998).